RECREATION AND THE SEA

EXETER MARITIME STUDIES

General Editors: Michael Duffy and David J. Starkey

Spanish Armada Prisoners: The Story of the Nuestra Señora del Rosario and her Crew and other Prisoners in England, 1587-97
by Paula Martin (1988)

Lisbon as a Port Town, the British Seaman and Other Maritime Themes
edited by Stephen Fisher (1988)

Devon's Coastline and Coastal Waters: Aspects of Man's Relationship with the Sea
edited by David J. Starkey (1988)

British Privateering Enterprise in the Eighteenth Century
by David J. Starkey (1990)

The Mary Fletcher: Seven Days in the Life of a Westcountry Coasting Ketch
by Edmund Eglinton, edited by Basil Greenhill (1990)

Innovation in Shipping and Trade
edited by Stephen Fisher (1989)

Parameters of British Naval Power, 1650-1850
edited by Michael Duffy (1992)

The Rise of the Devon Seaside Resorts, 1750-1900
by John Travis (1993)

Man and the Maritime Environment
edited by Stephen Fisher (1994)

Manila Ransomed: The British Assault on Manila in the Seven Years War
by Nicholas Tracy (1995)

Trawling: The Rise and Fall of the British Trawl Fishery
by Robb Robinson (1996)

Pirates and Privateers: New Perspectives on the War on Trade in the Eighteenth and Nineteenth Centuries
edited by David J. Starkey, E.S. van Eyck van Heslinga and J.A. de Moor (1997)

RECREATION AND THE SEA

Edited by

STEPHEN FISHER

UNIVERSITY
of
EXETER
PRESS

First published in 1997 by
University of Exeter Press
Reed Hall
Streatham Drive
Exeter EX4 4QR
UK

British Library Cataloguing in Publication Data

A catalogue record of this book is available from the British Library

ISBN 0 85989 540 8

Typeset in Palatino by Sue Milward

Printed in Great Britain by Short Run Press Ltd.

This volume is dedicated to my wife, Gertrud,
whose support and understanding in my
various academic and recreational pursuits
has long been inestimable.
(The Editor)

ACKNOWLEDGEMENTS

The editor wishes to express his thanks to Jane Ashby for her great skill and patience in word-processing this volume; to Helen Jones for her map-drawing talents; and to Sue Milward for her professional expertise in typesetting. Delphine Jones is to be congratulated on designing the book's cover. Finally, the editor is appreciative of the resourceful collaboration of Simon Baker and Richard Willis of the University Press in bringing this project to fruition.

Contents

Plates

Front Cover: Royal Western Yacht Club yachts off Mount's Bay,
                Cornwall, early October 1846 (*Illustrated London News*).

Figures

INTRODUCTION

Historical research into leisure and recreational activities, until comparatively recently a fairly neglected area of investigation, is now developing fast in Britain and elsewhere. This volume of papers arises from a national conference organised by the Centre for Maritime Historical Studies at Exeter University and held at Dartington Hall, Totnes, in October 1993. The conference focused on a specific theme of leisure and recreational studies, those related to the sea, the issues discussed comprising the historical evolution of sea-bathing, seaside tourism and yachting.

In a well-researched paper John Travis challenges the conventionally-held view of English sea-bathing in the Victorian age, which is that it was transformed through the fierce campaigns of moral crusaders into a restriction of both the traditional practice of male nude bathing and the equally old custom of the sexes bathing together. Dr Travis first discusses the mid-eighteenth century and earlier antecedents of English sea-bathing, the dual traditions of the fashionable 'taking the waters' – which at coastal resorts involved both 'dipping' in sea-water and even drinking the stuff – and folk or working class sea-bathing. His main concern though is to show that over the nineteenth century the commercial interests of many of the burgeoning English resorts in both attracting a clientele and granting it the freedom to bathe as it wished, despite the passing of by-laws, in actual practice triumphed over the campaigns of the moral reformers. By the 1890s there was a resurgence of mixed bathing and it was this that eventually brought male nude bathing to an end. The history of English sea-bathing is one of continuity as well as change: traditional practices were assailed by powerful forces but showed a remarkable ability to withstand the attack.

Three papers concern the development of that great modern expression of 'recreation and the sea', the seaside tourist resort. John Walton offers a pioneering overview of the rise of the continental Western European seaside resorts from their origins to the Second World War. He points out that their appearance was linked to the seaside resort's prior innovation in eighteenth-century England, providing yet another example of a significant English cultural export. Formal sea-bathing seasons and the attendant resorts emerged on the

French Channel coast from the late eighteenth century, being in part influenced by the developing English seaside resorts. The early emergence of the French resorts, including those of the French Riviera, was associated too with 'British seekers after cheapness, informality and the "lure" of abroad'.

Walton makes clear that this research area has received little attention as yet from Continental investigators, with the exception of some significant work on the French and Spanish resorts and, to a lesser extent, those of the Low Countries: his treatment therefore is necessarily broad and introductory. He seeks in part to explain the development of 'resort clusters' or local resort networks, and looks at three case studies of leading and successful resorts, Brighton in England, Nice in France and San Sebastián in Spain, to consider the disproportionate success of some resorts. He affirms that San Sebastián would have flourished more had it been more accessible to the two main streams of Continental cross-frontier holidaymakers, the British and the Germans. It is perhaps noteworthy that where the holidaymakers of these two nations went, tensions already seem to have been in evidence by the close of the nineteenth century, one Englishman in commenting on the Italian Riviera about Nervi noting that the growing 'Teutonic influence obtrudes itself unpleasantly at the hotel table d'hôte, sausages and an Italian form of sauerkraut being staple dishes'.[1] As Walton concludes, there is a rich agenda of European comparative research in seaside recreational studies waiting to be done.

Paul Thornton's contribution focuses on the late nineteenth-century rise and twentieth-century evolution of a leading British seaside resort region, that of Cornwall in the far south west of Britain. There were significant precursors of the Cornish seaside before 1900, Penzance, for example, offering itself as a health resort from about 1720, while Thomas Cook immediately exploited the railway's coming to Cornwall in 1859 by conducting his first excursion to the county in the same year. Dr Thornton, being essentially an economic geographer and therefore more influenced by theoretical models than most historians, has recourse to Butler's resort-cycle model, with its six 'product life-cycle' stages, from 'Exploration' to 'Post-Stagnation'; this latter stage offers a further five possibilities of evolution, ranging from 'Rejuvenation' to 'Catastrophic Decline'. In Thornton's view the evolution of Cornish seaside tourism can be characterised by this overall model, 'with deviations'. What the future holds at the turn of the twentieth century is, naturally enough, unclear. Our author though posits the view that it may be a case of developing the 'heritage tourism market', of attracting, ironically enough, the more affluent and discerning tourist which the Great Western Railway, a prime mover in both senses of Cornish tourism, was doing its best to attract in the century's early years. Thornton's paper is thoughtful and stands as one of the few overviews of Cornwall's seaside tourist history. Among its themes is the fascinating debate inaugurated by Sir Arthur Quiller-Couch in 1898 as to whether, and if so how, Cornwall should present itself as a tourist destination, a perennial debate it seems in that county.

The notion of a Cornish Riviera – conjuring up the French Riviera, with its elegant associations – was exploited very successfully by the Great Western Railway in its publicity in the early twentieth century. The seductive term 'Riviera' was also used by Torquay, the leading Devon resort in the inter-war years of this century, in its self-promotion as 'The Queen of the English Riviera', Torquay thus projecting itself as directly competing with southern French resorts such as Cannes. This ambition is well brought out by Nigel Morgan in his paper, a case-study in resort development strategy.

Dr Morgan indicates that the key players among the Devon resorts in the early twentieth century actively pursued policies to secure what they saw as their market position. Some, such as Ilfracombe, were aiming for a relatively broad market, while others, with Sidmouth in the van, by excluding certain types of tourist wished to preserve a more exclusive, genteel image. Torquay, however, was determined to straddle both camps. In the mid-nineteenth century it had an aristocratic-cum-gentry fashionable clientele; by the early twentieth century it had broadened its appeal by, among other things, various kinds of municipal entertainment. This move to a more popular resort continued in the inter-war years. Morgan considers the opinions within the town on how it should develop, particularly between those of the retired residents who wished to check down-market tendencies, and the hoteliers, caterers and motor coach operators who were in favour of expansion. The latter proved the more successful, and our author considers the resulting urban investment and other expenditures including the level of promotional spending, which was well ahead of the other Devon resorts although far behind the annual publicity budget of Blackpool, Britain's greatest seaside resort. In the inter-war period the town's promotional activities acquired an impressive professionalism, enabling it to sustain a 'popular fashionability'.

The last papers in this volume focus on the recreation of yachting, with both authors possessing perhaps a special insight into their subjects through being accomplished practitioners of the art. Janet Cusack reassesses, most interestingly and successfully, yachting's rise in England and South Devon, from the early seventeenth century to 1827. As she recognises, yachting offers more than the individual or team challenge and pleasure of most other sporting recreations. From its outset it has had a distinct social connotation, as a means, following Thorstein Veblen,[2] of asserting or claiming high social status through conspicuous consumption and display.

Dr Cusack modifies the traditional view that yachting, that is, pleasure sailing, and the word 'yacht' were introduced into England by Charles II in 1660 after his exile in Holland. She establishes that the term, spelt in its various forms, had an earlier usage at least two or three decades before, that royal pleasure sailing took place well before the Restoration, and that Charles II's interest in sailing predated the Civil War. Fascinating quotations from contemporary sources are presented, including one from the autobiography of Roger North, the lawyer, who, writing about a 1687 cruise, in a ten-ton yacht, caught well the delight of the pastime: '... we passed eight whole hours, and scarce knew what time was past ... no inconvenience to molest us, nor wants to trouble our thoughts, neither business to importune, nor formalities to tease us'.[3] The first documented cases of South Devon yachting date from the early eighteenth century, with the earliest yachts used, as was often the case earlier on the Thames and elsewhere, being Royal Navy vessels, while local noblemen such as the Courtenays of Powderham Castle and Sir Francis Drake of Nutwell, both on the Exe estuary, were prominent. Much evidence from different sources, public and private, is marshalled to document the story, including details of yacht numbers, size and rig, yachting costs and mode of use, and the early development of racing and regattas. Necessarily, because of the nature of the surviving records, Cusack's discussion concentrates on the larger yachts and, for the national scene, the early clubs and other institutional forms of behaviour. But, she properly cautions, we should not forget that, very largely unreported, was an unknown but possibly extensive practice of popular sailing, the scale of which occasionally peeps through the mists, particularly in newspaper reports. For instance, the *Exeter Flying Post*, in 1789, in reporting George III's visit to Plymouth, noted that 'their Majesties, in rowing up Catwater, received salutes and huzzas from upwards of 200 yatchs and pleasure boats',[4] a pretty remarkable number which would do credit to a royal visit even today.

Janet Cusack's paper reveals a distinct social exclusivity in yachting, at least in the sailing of the larger boats, to the early nineteenth century, which persisted through the century.[5] Our second yachting contribution, by Roger Ryan, on yachting in the North West of England from the later nineteenth century essentially to 1939 does, however, reveal some 'social broadening' in that it really deals with the rise of middle-class yachting, reflecting the thriving industrial and commercial hinterland. But, to 1939 at least, marked class distinctions, including gender discrimination, persisted.

In North West England in 1850 there were but three yacht clubs, the Royal Mersey Yacht Club, founded in 1844, and two other 'Royal' clubs, the Royal Dee and the Royal Welsh, all practising their sailing on the waters around Anglesey and in Liverpool Bay. By the early 1900s there were at least another sixteen regional clubs. These new creations fell under the regulatory aegis of the national Yacht Racing Association (YRA) founded in 1875, whose essential purpose apart from devising a system of racing time handicaps for boats of different sizes was to maintain, as Ryan puts it, a 'high standard of "gentlemanly" conduct upon the water and within clubhouses as participation in the sport widened', and as a result 'exclusiveness and social conformity' were retained. The YRA kept its control over sporting and social standards into the inter-war years. It was particularly opposed to 'artisan' or working class membership, although this 'obvious exclusiveness lost some of its edge' between the wars. Such influence was powerful indeed: in 1907, for instance, the newly-formed Blackpool and Fleetwood Sailing Club elected the Fleetwood lifeboat coxswain as a member, but when the YRA guidelines were brought to the club's notice the coxswain agreed to withdraw.

Dr Ryan offers a most interesting discussion of these social membership matters, including analysing the membership lists for the Royal Mersey Yacht Club and the West Lancashire Yacht Club to 1939. Women usually found full membership of the clubs closed, except in the role of 'Lady Members', with male attitudes towards yachtswomen before 1914 invariably appearing to the modern observer, as Ryan expresses it, 'extremely patronising'. He considers also the technical developments in smaller yachts over the period and especially the rise of the 'one-design' classes, which opened up membership somewhat by making yachting cheaper. It would appear that only since 1945 has yachting in the North West and elsewhere in England begun to relax its membership and gender lists. But this post-Second World War period gets little attention in this paper. It really deserves close study, as does the national yachting scene, which needs to be set in the long, historical social perspectives of yachting, to indicate (if it is the case) how socially revolutionary the post-1945 English yachting world really is.

The meeting which heard these sea-related recreational papers has proved to be the last in a long series of maritime history research conferences held at Dartington Hall, Totnes under the sponsorship of the Department of Economic History and latterly the Centre for Maritime Historical Studies at Exeter University. These annual Dartington events, dating from October 1967, originally focused on the maritime history of the South West of England, but moved into wider national and international waters, as the research publications in the series *Exeter Papers in Economic History* and subsequently *Exeter Maritime Studies* show.[6] A persisting feature of these Dartington conferences was, it is generally agreed, the stimulating mix of the participants, drawn from diverse academic, professional, business and other backgrounds, some with a direct experience of the sea, professional or otherwise, others merely fascinated by it. The conferences have now – through circumstances beyond the organisers' control – relocated to the University's Crossmead Conference Centre in Exeter. It is hoped they will continue to be as lively, congenial and productive as those held in the delightful setting of Dartington Hall. The editor of this volume, on behalf of all past Dartington conference members, takes this opportunity to thank the staff of Dartington Hall, and particularly the long-time Warden of the Devon Centre, Tom Griffiths, for their much-esteemed support and many kindnesses.

June 1996   Stephen Fisher

NOTES

1   One is reminded of the recent appearance in numbers of Russian holidaymakers in the Mediterranean, with some Cypriot hotels, long dominated by visitors from the island's former colonial power, now listing Chicken Kiev and bortsch on their menus (though apparently without any accompanying tension). *The Times*, 29 March 1996, p.23.
2   Thorstein Veblen, *The Theory of the Leisure Class: An Economic Study of Institutions* (New York, 1931 edn.).
3   A. Jessop, ed., *The Autobiography of the Hon. Roger North* (London, 1887).
4   *Exeter Flying Post*, 20 August 1789.
5   See her unpublished University of Exeter PhD thesis, 'The Rise of Aquatic Recreation and Sport: Yachting and Rowing in England and South Devon, 1640-1914' (1996).

6   The list, published by the University of Exeter Press, is as follows
(edited in all cases by H.E.S./Stephen Fisher, with the exception
of *Transport and Shipowning in the West Country*, jointly edited by
Fisher and Walter E. Minchinton): *The South West and the Sea*
(1968), pp.73; *Ports and Shipping in the South-West* (1970), pp. x +
174; *Transport and Shipowning in the West Country* (1973), pp. iv +
83; *West Country Maritime and Social History: Some Essays* (1980),
pp. ix + 159; *British Shipping and Seamen, 1630-1960: Some Studies*
(1984), pp. xii + 109; *Studies in British Privateering, Trading
Enterprise and Seamen's Welfare, 1775-1900* (1987), pp. xiii + 165;
Lisbon as a Port Town, the British Seaman and other Maritime Themes
(1988), pp. vi + 143; *Innovation in Shipping and Trade* (1989), pp. vi
+ 177; *Man and the Maritime Environment* (1994), pp. x + 233.

CONTINUITY AND CHANGE IN ENGLISH SEA-BATHING, 1730-1900:
A CASE OF SWIMMING WITH THE TIDE

John Travis

Change has been the issue preoccupying the historians who have written about sea-bathing on the English coast. Most commentators have suggested that sea-bathing was transformed in the nineteenth century following a sustained attack by moral crusaders. They have noted that the local authorities at the seaside resorts enacted by-laws prohibiting the traditional practice of male nude bathing and the equally old custom of the sexes bathing together. Then they have assumed that these by-laws were enforced firmly and decisively. This had led them to the conclusion that the time-honoured ways of bathing must have been completely stamped out.[1]

This paper will challenge this interpretation. It will present evidence to show that, despite fierce attacks, the old sea-bathing practices managed to survive at many coastal resorts. Changes certainly took place, but the paper will suggest they were much more gradual than has previously been claimed. It will show that both nude bathing and mixed bathing survived at many resorts long after their total eradication had been proclaimed. In essence, I will be arguing that the history of English sea-bathing is one of continuity as well as change.

The Antecedents of Fashionable Sea-Bathing

When sea-bathing first became fashionable in the mid-eighteenth century it was thought to be an innovation, but in fact it drew heavily on tradition, having its origins in two quite different customs. One of these customs had developed in the late sixteenth century when a few fashionable members of society began to visit spa towns such as Bath and Buxton.[2] 'Taking the waters' was the term used to describe a stay at a spa, because the visitors hoped to improve their health by bathing in the mineral water and drinking it. The spas were often referred to as 'watering places'. This tradition of visiting the spas played an important part in the development of sea-bathing on the English coast. The first seaside resorts were also referred to as 'watering places' because visitors to them likewise bathed in the water and drank it. At the coastal resorts, however, it was sea-water rather than spa water which was thought to be a panacea.

The bathing ritual at these early seaside resorts was closely modelled on time-honoured practices at the inland watering places. Bathers rarely swam. Instead they were dipped under the waves as if they were taking a medicinal bath. 'Dippers' were employed to submerge bathers under water. The seaside resorts emulated the spas by making similarly exaggerated claims of miraculous cures for those who 'took the waters'. Teignmouth, for example, boasted in 1762:

> For the sake of drinking that fashionable purging draught, sea water, and bathing ... numbers of people from all parts resort here in the summer season, and cripples frequently recover the use of their limbs, hysterical ladies their spirits and even the lepers are cleansed.[3]

Continuities with the spas were also evident in the social institutions provided by the early coastal resorts. Their sea-water baths, assembly rooms, circulating libraries and promenades were closely modelled on facilities provided at their precursors. The seaside resorts hoped that these amenities would enable them to attract an equally wealthy clientele.

The second custom from which fashionable sea-bathing stemmed was that of working people visiting the coast to bathe in the sea. A paucity of documentary evidence makes it difficult to determine when this folk activity began, but certainly by the eighteenth century it was an established practice at several places on the English coast. Lancashire was one county with a tradition of popular therapeutic sea-bathing. Walton has shown that it was definitely being practised there by 1709, when a Crosby man had his two daughters dipped in the sea to cure a skin complaint.[4] Later in the eighteenth century there are a number of references suggesting that Lancashire artisans and country folk had long been accustomed to make annual journeys to the coast in order to bathe.[5] From Liverpool, for example, it was reported that prior to the War of American Independence thousands of 'country people' from distant inland districts had gone there to sea-bathe, but that during the war fear of the press gang had caused numbers to drop.[6] There is, of course, a possibility that these Lancashire people were following the example of their social superiors, but the scale of these annual migrations to the coast makes it much more likely that they were the survival of an older custom.

Plate 1. Sea-bathing at Bridlington, 1813. Bathers were dipped under the waves by attendants. (Reproduced by kind permission of the East Riding of Yorkshire Council)

These Lancashire working people bathed naked in the sea, without any segregation of the sexes. In 1795 one observer described how the 'lower class of people, of both sexes' made an annual pilgrimage from the inland towns to Liverpool, where they could be seen 'dabbling in the salt-water for hours at each tide, covering the beach with their promiscuous numbers and not much embarrassing themselves about appearances'.[7]

There is also evidence of popular sea-bathing in Sussex. In 1752 Dr Richard Russell explained, in his seminal book, *Dissertation on the Uses of Sea Water in the Diseases of the Glands*, that he had only begun to recommend the therapeutic advantages of sea-bathing to his wealthy patients after he had observed that the ordinary inhabitants of Sussex coastal villages 'made use of sea-water' to treat ailments.[8]

There may also have been a folk tradition of sea-bathing on the South Devon coast. In 1750 Bishop Pococke visited Exmouth, which was situated in what was then a remote part of England, where fashionable influences would have been slow to penetrate. Pococke described the estuarine village as 'a place to which the people of Exeter much resort for diversion and bathing in the sea'.[9] It seems significant that this earliest surviving reference to sea-bathing on the Devon coast used the phrase 'the people of Exeter', for this suggests the general citizenry rather than a small minority of Exeter gentry and merchants.

Supporting evidence for this interpretation of the word 'people' comes from the journal of Samuel Curwen, who visited Exmouth in 1779. He again referred to 'Exeter people' who arrived 'in shoals' each summer weekend. These must have been ordinary people with little to spend, for Curwen writes that their visits to Exmouth were 'not ... to the emolument or wish of the inhabitants to whom they are of no advantage'. By this time Exmouth was also playing host to a few wealthy visitors from more distant parts of England. Curwen made a point of contrasting the genteel behaviour of these rich strangers with that of the 'shoals of Exeter damsels, whose insufferable undress and ill-breeding' exposed them 'to the contempt and derision of strangers'.[10]

There is also a fragment of evidence suggesting there may have been a tradition of popular therapeutic sea-bathing at Southampton. When the poet Thomas Gray visited the infant resort in 1764 he wrote: 'My health is much improved by the sea, not that I drank it or bathed in it as the common people do.'[11]

The evidence therefore suggests that when sea-bathing became a fashionable leisure pursuit in the second half of the eighteenth century, it incorporated elements of long-established bathing customs drawn from the experience of working people as well as the leisured class. This finding has significance when related to the wider context of the history of leisure. In recent years a few historians have begun to consider whether some forms of organised sport and commercial entertainment might have originated within popular culture and subsequently been adopted by the upper and middle classes, rather than being initiated high up the social scale and only later filtering down to the working classes.[12] Sea-bathing is relevant to this discussion as an example of a leisure activity which appears to have had an input from below as well as from above.

Fashionable Sea-Bathing in the Eighteenth Century

As early as 1718 there is a reference to sea-bathing of the fashionable kind at Whitby. A poem was published telling how a gentleman had visited the Yorkshire fishing village and had been cured of jaundice by the 'drinking of Whitby spaw waters'. The poet recommended others to 'take the waters' at Whitby and declared: 'What the drinking cannot purge away is cured with ease by dipping in the sea.'[13]

Whitby was only a minor spa but further south on the Yorkshire coast was the much more important spa resort of Scarborough, and from there in the early 1730s came reports of fashionable sea-bathing. In May 1732 the *Universal Spectator* stated that it was 'usual for the ladies to bathe here publicly and frequently in the sea'. In 1734 a visitor to Scarborough wrote that it was 'the custom here for not only the gentlemen, but also the ladies, to bathe in the sea'.[14] These early references to fashionable sea-bathing at Whitby and Scarborough point to continuity with the custom of 'taking the waters' at the spas. At both Whitby and Scarborough the mineral spring issued from the base of a cliff, so it was only a short step across the beach to the sea. After sampling the spa waters, a few visitors must have decided to see if a dip in the sea would improve their health.

By 1736 a few members of the leisured class were sea-bathing at both Margate and Brighton.[15] By 1750 the start of a fashionable sea-bathing season had also been noted at Deal, Eastbourne, Portsmouth and Exmouth.[16] Later in the century sea-bathing became all the rage. Members of the middle class began to join the aristocracy and gentry at the seaside. To cater for this growing demand, seaside resorts began to emerge at many more places on the English coast.

It was the search for better health which first persuaded some members of the leisured class to take up sea-bathing. The medical profession advised bathers to dip before ten in the morning so that the cold water would invigorate the constitution for the rest of the day.

Few swam; most were dipped into the 'healing brine' by brawny bathing attendants (see Plate 1). This could be an unpleasant experience, especially for those of a nervous disposition. Indeed it almost seems as though sea-bathing was deliberately made as unpleasant as possible, on the principle that the more disagreeable the treatment, the more likely the chance of a cure.

One significant feature of eighteenth-century fashionable sea-bathing was that gentlemen and boys almost always bathed naked. Wearing bathing drawers was regarded as a sign of effeminacy. Males also thought that a costume would prevent them obtaining the full benefit of having saline water next to their skin. In bathing naked these gentlemen were adopting a custom long practised by working people. Ladies and girls, however, usually wore flannel gowns when in the sea. A few early pictures show members of the fair sex bathing naked, but if this was not simply artistic licence then it was an unusual practice. Contemporary accounts make it clear that, while working women often bathed naked, those from the middle and upper ranks of society almost always wore dresses when in the sea.

Take the case of Scarborough: pictures of 1735 and 1813 show females bathing naked in the sea,[17] but contemporary observers made a point of stating that the ladies wore costumes while bathing. In 1732, when sea-bathing was in its infancy, a poet at Scarborough enthused over the 'charming maids' clad in 'kindly-clinging' garments while dipping in the sea.[18] Two years later another early writer noted that, while the gentlemen at Scarborough bathed in the nude, the women had the 'conveniency of gowns'.[19] Later in the century there are a number of references to ladies wearing flannel dresses while sea-bathing at Scarborough,[20] as there are for other seaside resorts.

Bathing machines were introduced in the mid-eighteenth century. In them bathers could change and then be transported down to the sea, safe from prying eyes. In reality they were little more than huts on wheels, which were hauled up and down the foreshore by bathing attendants or horses according to the dictates of the tide. Bathing machines were certainly in use at Margate and Deal by 1753.[21] Other resorts were quick to follow: Ramsgate and Broadstairs, for example, introduced them at the beginning of the 1754 season. Brighton likewise had 'carriages for the conveniency of bathing' by 1754.[22]

Another important feature of eighteenth-century fashionable sea-bathing was that the sexes normally bathed in the same section of the sea, just as men and women of the lower classes had long done. 'Promiscuous bathing' was the name usually given to the practice, but in this period few members of polite society found anything wrong in it. On first consideration this might seem surprising in view of the fact that the gentlemen were naked when bathing. However, it has to be remembered that in this early period visitor numbers were small, so bathers were not crowded together. What is more, few fashionable bathers swam, most were simply dipped, and this meant that they had few opportunities to meet members of the opposite sex while in the water. Once bathing machines were introduced, most bathers stayed close to their machines while being immersed.

At a few seaside resorts half-hearted attempts were made to segregate the sexes. At Brighton it seems that there was an attempt to introduce a system of zoning, for in 1768 a Dr Awsiter wrote that he *thought* the shore to the east of the town had been 'allotted to the use of the ladies without any mixture of gentlemen'. However, he went on to write of the need for a further rule stating that 'no man-servant or inhabitant be permitted to bathe on that side of the town'.[23] This suggests that the division was ignored by many bathers. At Blackpool, there was an attempt to segregate the sexes by operating a time system. In 1789 one visitor reported that a bell was rung when it was time for first the ladies and then the gentlemen to bathe in the sea. However, the system depended on honour rather than any formal regulations, with gentlemen being expected to forfeit a bottle of wine if they were seen on the parade while the ladies were bathing.[24]

Such segregation was the exception rather than the rule. At most seaside resorts the sexes continued sea-bathing together in a state of 'happy innocence'. At Sidmouth, for example, one diarist recorded in 1797: 'There are but four machines employed and the gentlemen and ladies engage them indiscriminately.'[25] Even at resorts where the men and women were allocated separate bathing machines, little or no effort seems to have been made to locate these machines on separate parts of the beach, so the sexes usually bathed together in the sea. The regulation of behaviour was usually left to the good sense of the participants. There was not a perceived need for local legislation to enforce a code of conduct on those who sea-bathed.

The Nineteenth Century: Traditional Sea-Bathing Practices Face Attack

As the eighteenth century came to an end, attitudes began to change and traditional sea-bathing practices came under attack. In September 1800 the *Observer* denounced the method of bathing at the English seaside resorts:

> The indecency of numerous naked men bathing in the sea close to the ladies' bathing machines, and under the windows of the principal houses at most of the watering places has long been complained of, but in general has not been ... redressed.[26]

Complaints about 'indecent' sea-bathing steadily increased. At Worthing, for example, in 1805 a local guide book declared that the lack of a proper division between the sexes while bathing was 'indecent and inconsistent with the rules of propriety and morality'.[27] Likewise at Southport in 1824 one visitor protested that sea-bathing was 'sadly exposing'. She went on to say: 'The modest complain much, gentlemen's and ladies' machines standing promiscuously in the water.'[28]

Seaside resorts were slow to respond to the mounting pressure. Males were still allowed to bathe nude. By the 1830s some resorts had designated separate sections of the beach for ladies and gentlemen to bathe from, but there were few attempts to enforce a segregation of the sexes while in the sea. It was in the 1850s and 1860s that traditional sea-bathing practices came under really fierce attack from well-organised pressure groups. Every time the summer sea-bathing season began, both the local and national newspapers called attention to the 'disgraceful scenes' as shameless bathers cavorted in the sea.[29]

There were a number of reasons for the mounting concern, some relating to people's attitudes and some to the changing nature of sea-bathing itself. Prudery was an important factor, for it was frightening away the innocence of an earlier age. The Evangelicals were in the ascendancy and they regarded both nudity and mixed bathing as immoral. Others, more concerned with external propriety than with internal piety, fostered the cult of respectability, believing that by placing stress on the social niceties they would gain social status. Then there were some who believed that a woman's place was in the home and thought she compromised her position by appearing in public places in mixed company, particularly in a state of semi-undress. There were also those who tried to draw a veil over the realities of life, wanting to cover up those parts of the body concerned with excretion and reproduction.

These opponents of traditional bathing condemned those who bathed in the old way as hypocrites. They pointed out that in any other situation these bathers would have been horrified at the thought of exposing any part of their bodies to public view, and yet once at the seaside they happily shed all their clothes and inhibitions. In July 1865 the *Observer* thundered:

Under ordinary circumstances English ladies and gentlemen keep within the bounds or propriety – not so at watering places. In those places no sooner do they arrive than they seem to give up their decorum with their rail or boat ticket and to adopt practices which at home they would shudder even to read of.[30]

The attack on traditional bathing practices was also prompted by a fundamental change in the bathing ritual. In earlier years the daily dip had been regarded as a necessary ordeal for the improvement of health rather than as an enjoyable pastime. Few bathers had strayed far from the machines; they had remained in the sea only long enough to be dipped by attendants. All that changed when swimming became fashionable in the mid-nineteenth century. Now some members of the fair sex began to venture away from the privacy of the rear of the bathing machine and actually began to swim or wade about in the sea. Most women wore long flannel bathing gowns, but while these were tied with a string around the neck they were left unfastened at the bottom, so they were quite unsuitable for swimming in.[31] In August 1856 a reporter for the *Observer* went onto the crowded beaches at Ramsgate and Margate and saw that the sea was 'black with bathers'. He wrote:

Females do not venture beyond the surf and lay themselves on their backs, waiting for the coming waves, with their bathing dresses in a most *dégagée* style. The waves come and ... carry their dresses up to their neck, so that, as far as decency is concerned, they might as well be without any dresses at all ... And all this takes place in the presence of thousands of spectators ... in fact it is looked upon much as a scene at a play would be, as the gentlemen are there with their opera glasses.[32]

The problem was thought to be even more serious in the case of the gentlemen, for most still insisted on bathing nude. Once males were no longer content with being dipped next to their machine, but began to swim, it was inevitable that by accident or design they would encounter female bathers. In August 1859 the *Observer* reported from Ramsgate:

There is not even the slightest pretension to common decency. The men gambol about in a complete state of nature, and the ladies frolic in very questionable bathing garments within a few yards of them, while the sands are crowded with spectators of the scenes, of all ages and both sexes.[33]

A third reason for the mounting concern about sea-bathing was the increasing pressure on space in the bathing area. Rising real incomes and transport improvements were enabling more people to holiday at the seaside and, as the number of bathers increased, so the problems of nudity and 'promiscuous' bathing seemed much more serious than in the days when there had only been a few bathers. The situation was made worse at high tide, for then space was reduced still further and the bathers were forced close to the promenades in full view of the spectators.

A fourth factor was the arrival on the beach of growing numbers of working-class excursionists. These day-trippers lacked the money to hire bathing machines and seemed quite unaware of the local bathing conventions. It was quite common for these visitors to strip off on the beach, and men and women alike ran naked into the sea. Long-stay visitors were shocked by such behaviour. The case of Dawlish (see Plate 2) illustrates this point. In 1858 Dr Miller, an Exeter doctor, persuaded the South Devon Railway to offer a six-penny return fare from Exeter so that the poor could benefit from a dip in the sea. To try to avoid upsetting the social élite at the resort, the railway company stipulated that the new cheap fare would only be available to those who travelled on the first train down and caught the first train back. This allowed the bathers a maximum of only one hour and ten minutes in Dawlish, barely sufficient time for a dip, but quite long enough to scandalise the beach! The genteel residents were quick to complain of the 'indecent' behaviour of these 'six-penny dippers'. So these bathing excursions, which were thought to be highly improving at the point of departure, were regarded as a serious threat by the seaside resort which had to receive them.[34]

It could be argued that this hostility towards working-class bathers was an attempt by the middle and upper classes to appropriate an area which had been public space. The foreshore had traditionally been a communal area, but now some members of the ruling élite at the seaside resorts wanted to reserve the bathing ground for the exclusive use of the socially acceptable. They tried to prevent people bathing who could not afford to use bathing machines, or would not conform to the conventions of the resort. This can be viewed as part of a nationwide struggle over the use of space, with the wealthier sections of society trying to demarcate areas for their

Plate 2. The ladies' bathing beach at Dawlish, c.1870. Gentlemen were expected to bathe in a secluded cove beyond the first headland. (Reproduced by kind permission of Andrew Farmer)

private use on land which had always been regarded as common and public.[35]

The 1860s: By-Laws Proliferate

Faced with such a strong body of protest, the ruling élite at the English seaside resorts felt obliged to seek new powers of prohibition and restraint, so that they could be seen to be taking steps to regulate sea-bathing. Yet it was also apparent that those in authority would have to tread carefully, for many visitors secretly preferred the traditional way of bathing.

The debate at the seaside resorts centred on moral and commercial issues. The usual scenario was for a small but vociferous group of moral reformers to lobby hard for by-laws to be brought in to ban both nude and mixed bathing, but for commercial interests to urge caution because of the risk of losing a substantial number of visitors. Take the case of Scarborough. In the summer of 1866 the *Scarborough Gazette* received several letters complaining that males were bathing naked. One claimed that this turned a healthy recreation into 'an immoral and depraved exhibition'.[36] Another ridiculed those who said that nude bathing should be allowed to continue because it was an 'ancient practice'. This letter declared that 'the vast increase in the number of visitors ... rendered the evil tenfold greater than in former times'.[37] In September of that year the Scarborough Town Council received two petitions objecting to 'indecent' bathing: one from the clergy of the town and one from a number of local inhabitants. While both these petitions emphasised 'the higher grounds of morality and public decency', it was significant that they also found it necessary to refer to 'pecuniary considerations'. One petition claimed that families were 'withdrawing' from Scarborough because they were shocked at the 'indecent' behaviour of the bathers and so 'the interests of the town as a watering place' were being damaged.[38]

The Scarborough nude-bathing issue had been raised by the moral reformers, but the resulting debate often centred on commercial considerations. Those concerned about immorality argued that, if 'indecent' bathing was not stopped, the resort would lose its good reputation and the more respectable visitors would be driven away. Yet the proprietors of the bathing machines, who were in the best position to know their customers' needs, put in a counter petition to the Council stating: 'We know from experience that first-class visitors object to wearing drawers when bathing ... and if obliged to wear drawers ... Scarborough will necessarily lose its fame for want of good families who have hitherto come here to bathe according to ancient usage.'[39] The two sides sometimes tried to appropriate the high ground of their opponents' arguments. The moral reformers claimed that 'disgraceful' bathing scenes were causing a loss of trade because parents were taking their children away from the resort, and husbands their wives, rather than allow them to see 'indecent' bathing take place. Business interests argued that it would be morally wrong to bring in by-laws that would deprive the poorer classes of the chance to bathe, because they could not afford to hire a bathing costume.[40]

The Scarborough Town Council's main concern seems to have been to keep the patronage of as many of the resort's patrons as possible, so it came up with a compromise which went some way towards appeasing the reformers without damaging the summer sea-bathing trade. The Council introduced a by-law stating that in the main bathing area, in front of the spa, the men must wear drawers, except before seven in the morning and after nine at night. Elsewhere they could continue to bathe in the time-honoured way, that is without a costume. The Council justified its decision to allow nude bathing from the less central beaches on the grounds that this would 'prevent the entire exclusion of the labouring classes and others who may be unable to provide themselves with drawers', but it was also ensuring that there were sections of beach from which better-class bathers could bathe without a costume.[41]

All along the English coast there were similar demands for legislation to stamp out naked sea-bathing and to make males and females bathe separately.[42] Local authorities felt obliged to take action to appease those campaigning for reform. The result was a welter of new by-laws.

Indeed it was often the need for more effective controls over sea-bathing which prompted many small seaside resorts, previously without an effective form of local government, to obtain the powers of a Local Board so that they could bring in new by-laws. On the Devon coast, for example, Dawlish in 1859 sought the powers of a Local Board to prevent the excesses of the 'six-penny dippers'.[43] Sidmouth in 1863 established a Local Board after complaints about 'shameless men going stark naked in and out of the sea when a number of girls are waiting for the machines'.[44] Likewise when Seaton in 1877 applied to form a Local Board, it gave as one of its principal reasons that, 'in consequence of there being no local authority for the place, disgraceful and indecent scenes' were 'frequently occurring'.[45]

The flood of new by-laws might have been expected to bring a speedy end to the traditional sea-bathing practices. However, this was not the case. My research shows that the old ways persisted at many resorts because the authorities were frightened to prosecute offenders, in the knowledge that many of their wealthy patrons actually preferred the traditional way of bathing. The problem was not the lack of legislation but the lack of will to rigorously enforce it. The case of Brighton illustrates the point. This proud resort had been one of the first to bring in legislation to regulate sea-bathing. As early as 1807 the vestry had passed a series of resolutions decreeing that on the main beach bathing would only be allowed from machines.[46] Then in August 1825 the Brighton Commissioners brought in by-laws designating separate areas for the ladies' and gentlemen's machines.[47] By 1865 the resort had by-laws stating that after seven in the morning nobody should bathe from these machines without being suitably clad.[48] Here then was a seaside resort with a strict bathing code which was often held up as a model for other resorts to emulate.[49] Yet on examination it is clear that at Brighton, as elsewhere, the by-laws were openly flouted. In September 1865 an *Observer* reporter visited the resort and found the 'men in a state of nature and ladies with apologies of covering ... exposed to the stare and remarks of the crowds who lined the beach'.[50]

Margate was another resort which brought in by-laws to regulate sea-bathing, but then failed to enforce them. In 1862 a newspaper campaign[51] finally obliged the Town Council to introduce legislation decreeing that 'a distance of not less than sixty feet shall be preserved ... between the bathing machines from which females are bathing and those from which males are bathing', and that all bathers must wear 'drawers, or a gown or dress, or other such suitable clothing as shall prevent any indecent exposure of the person'.[52] Margate now had strict bathing regulations, but was still not prepared to prosecute offenders. In July 1863 a letter to the *Thanet Advertiser* pointed out that Margate's new by-laws were being ignored, with the bathers still bathing 'in like manner as before, despite all the fulminations of the dignitaries big and little'.[53] Two years later the *Observer* complained that men were bathing naked in the presence of ladies and declared that this showed the by-laws were 'mere waste paper'.[54] In September 1866 the same newspaper resumed its attack, pointing out that the sexes were still bathing together at Margate and most men were swimming in the nude:

> The regulations, we admit, are excellent, only they are not carried out. Where one man uses bathing drawers, ten do not ... The authorities are openly set at defiance, and for

the simple reason that offenders know they will not prosecute.[55]

The *Pall Mall Gazette* suggested another reason why the local authorities at the seaside resorts were reluctant to put a stop to the traditional bathing practices. It claimed they feared losing the patronage of those holiday-makers who enjoyed watching the antics of naked bathers:

> At every seaside resort there is to be found a class of visitors of both sexes, of whose presence and custom the tradespeople and lodging-house keepers are unwilling to be deprived, who derive a prurient gratification and employment in gazing on the naked and half-naked forms of the bathers.[56]

The *Pall Mall Gazette* had a point. Visitors certainly congregated wherever naked bathing took place. In the summer of 1865, for example, the *Observer* complained about the crowds which gathered at Ramsgate and Brighton at each high tide 'to witness the shameless exposure and indelicate practice of those disporting in the sea'.[57] The same newspaper also noted that at Margate ladies outraged 'decorum by viewing from the pier and the beach, through opera glasses, the antics of nude gentlemen'.[58]

Although the moral reformers issued dire warnings that fathers would remove their wives and daughters from these 'scenes of immorality',[59] there was precious little evidence to support their view. Complaints in the press seemed to make little difference to a resort's trade. Indeed the publicity may well have brought in more trade than was lost.

It was only when day-trippers blatantly infringed the bathing by-laws that a few local authorities occasionally felt the need to take action. A seaside resort with an elevated 'social tone' might feel obliged to make a scapegoat of a working-class bather, partly to appease the moral reformers but more to placate those long-stay patrons who objected to their wives having to encounter naked labourers and artisans in the sea. Even then there would be no attempt to follow up one successful prosecution with a series of others.

By the mid-1860s a clear pattern had emerged. The seaside resorts were trying to be 'all things to all people'. They sought compromise rather than conflict, attempting to placate the Evangelicals and 'respectables' without upsetting those visitors who wished to bathe in the time-honoured way. By this time most resorts had designated separate areas of the beach for males and females to enter the sea, and now they were busy bringing in new by-laws which were supposed to stop both nude bathing and the sexes mixing in the ocean. Yet, as we have seen, the market mattered more than morality at most seaside resorts. While the ruling élite tried to maintain a veneer of respectability, they were not prepared fully to enforce their legislation for fear of driving away many of their best-paying customers. In 1866 the *Pall Mall Gazette* made the point very clearly:

> From time to time, whenever the interests of a particular locality seems to be threatened by the discreditable notoriety thus conferred upon its beach, by-laws are enacted and published for the more rigid observance of delicacy ... but the very same feeling of self-interest which calls for these by-laws invariably interposes to prevent their being enforced.[60]

The 1890s: Survival and Revival

Old customs die hard, and both nude bathing and mixed bathing persisted right up to the end of the century at many places on the English coast. They survived but not unchanged. Adjustments and adaptations had to be made in the face of continued attack. By the 1890s male nude bathing and mixed bathing no longer took place at the same place and time. Furthermore, both practices had been marginalised; forced to retreat to smaller seaside resorts, or to the edges of the bigger watering places, or to be confined to the beginning and end of the day. Yet they still continued long after their eradication had been proclaimed.

In the 1890s there were still many places where men and boys could sea-bathe in the nude. 'At most English resorts,' declared the *Cosmopolitan* in 1895, 'buff bathing is permitted before eight o'clock in the morning'.[61] Resorts such as Brighton, Worthing, Hastings, Bexhill, Bognor and Folkestone still tolerated male nude bathing at any time of day in areas away from the central bathing areas.[62] At Hastings, for example, it was reported in 1899 that at each end of the beach there was a place where men could still bathe 'in the fearless old fashion'.[63] Phrases such as this indicated that some still felt the old custom was worth defending. 'For a man to thoroughly enjoy a sea bath,' declared one letter to the *Daily Graphic* in September 1895, 'he must be perfectly free and untrammelled from any kind of costume whatsoever'.[64] The seaside resorts remained reluctant to enforce their by-laws while some affluent visitors still held this view.

On the subject of mixed bathing misconceptions abound. Pimlott, for example, has suggested that in the second half of the nineteenth century the sexes were always strictly segregated while sea-bathing, and that Bexhill in 1901 was one of the first seaside resorts to reintroduce mixed bathing.[65] Other commentators have recycled this erroneous information and have referred to Bexhill as a progressive trendsetting resort.[66] Nothing could be further from the truth. In 1896 it was reported that males and females were bathing together at places as far apart as Newquay, Felixstowe, Littlehampton, Deal, Seaton, Barmouth, Tenby and Sea View on the Isle of Wight.[67] At most of these resorts mixed bathing was more a survival than a revival. Even at the English resorts where mixed bathing had to be reintroduced, we shall see that this began in the late 1890s rather than early in the twentieth century. Far from leading the movement, Bexhill was well back in the field.

Yet perhaps it is hardly surprising that most present-day commentators have failed to realise that mixed bathing continued in the late-Victorian period; even at the time, some people were unaware that there were still places where the sexes could bathe in the sea together. After numerous letters about sea-bathing had appeared in the *Daily Graphic* in the summer of 1895, one correspondent pointed out that most letter-writers had wrongly assumed that there were 'but one or two spots where the sexes can mingle in the water, or none at all'. He stated emphatically that this was not the case and that men and women bathed 'together in almost every part of the country except at the larger resorts'.[68]

This was a valid comment, for mixed bathing was still widespread. However, we need to qualify the point. In the mid-1890s it was only the very small seaside resorts, and a handful of moderate-sized ones, which still allowed mixed bathing from their main beaches. At the great majority of resorts, the central beaches were carefully split up into male and female bathing areas. Yet just away from the central beaches, even at select resorts such as Eastbourne,[69] men and women quite often swam together, because outside the town boundaries there was no local authority with the power or will to prevent it.

In August 1896, the *Daily Mail* called attention to the absurdity of the mixed-bathing situation at the English seaside resorts. It instanced the case of Margate, where on the main beach printed notices declared that male and female bathers must keep to their designated bathing areas, while at one end of the resort, just outside the domain of the town council, 'men and maids' could 'swim in company without any sense of indecorum'. The same newspaper pointed out: 'In many of the smaller bathing towns, where there are no bathing machines and possibly no town councils, family bathing parties are the rule.'[70]

From 1895 a strong campaign was mounted to reintroduce mixed bathing on the main beaches at those seaside resorts where it was not allowed. Petitions were organised and local newspapers were bombarded with letters demanding a relaxation of the bathing regulations. The *Daily Graphic, Standard, Daily Mail* and *Daily Telegraph* spearheaded this campaign, writing long editorials and encouraging a lively correspondence in their columns.[71] In 1896 the *Daily Mail* even organised petitions at a number of coastal resorts.[72] Here were signs of a significant change in attitude, for in earlier years many newspapers had argued forcibly for a stricter bathing code. The moral reformers fought a strong rearguard action, but most strands of public opinion now demanded that the bathing regulations be relaxed rather than tightened.

One of the main arguments put forward by the supporters of mixed bathing was that segregated bathing split up the family. By the late Victorian era the growing popularity of family holidays had made the beach a natural playground for the young and old of both sexes, and it was not surprising that families should want to be together when they entered the sea. Ridicule was poured on the rules which separated husband and wife, father and daughter, brother and sister while bathing.[73]

Some claimed that fewer women and girls would drown at the seaside if the menfolk could go into the sea with them and teach them how to swim.[74] It was certainly true that never a summer passed without reports of tragic bathing accidents; it was also true that many women and girls had never been taught to swim. 'Who is better fitted,' asked a letter to the *Daily Graphic* in September 1895, 'to teach a timid wife and daughter to swim than the man whose home they adorn?'[75]

In August 1895 the *Cosmopolitan* pointed to another absurdity of segregated bathing: 'The beach ... is often crowded with men and women watching the bathing. As a practical result, therefore, as far as any seclusion or privacy is concerned, the bathers might just as well use the same grounds.'[76]

Many people began to call attention to Continental seaside resorts, such as Trouville, Dieppe and Boulogne, where mixed bathing was accepted and asked why similar bathing opportunities should not be available at all the English seaside resorts.[77] In June 1896, for instance, a letter in the *Standard* pointed out that 'on the Continent men and women bathe together and there is nothing to shock the sensibilities of the most prudish'.[78] The reason for this was that at these Continental resorts both men and women wore neck-to-knee costumes. There was general agreement that those English resorts which reintroduced mixed bathing would have to insist on similar bathing costumes.

It was also pointed out that single-sex bathing was often a solitary and joyless ritual whereas mixed bathing could be fun. 'The Briton takes his pleasures sadly', declared the *Daily Graphic* in August 1895 in an editorial on sea-bathing.[79] In the following year the *Blackpool Herald* made a similar point when it suggested that segregated bathing was 'a rather lonely and cheerless function'. It claimed:

> Where friends and families are allowed to bathe together the dip is a pleasant social function ... thousands of people who would fail to find any enjoyment in a solitary plunge are induced to enter the water for the sake of the frolic and mirth that accompany the process of immersion.[80]

Comments like this make it clear that pleasure was replacing health as the principal reason for taking a holiday.

The pressure to change the outdated bathing regulations mounted but, as always, the ruling élite at the seaside resorts were reluctant to initiate change. Once again their decisions were mainly motivated by commercial rather than moral considerations. Seaside resorts only began officially to reintroduce mixed bathing when they were convinced that they would lose trade to other more progressive British or Continental resorts if they resisted the demand for change. Usually, it was the resorts with sandy beaches which were the first to bring back mixed bathing, for they depended far more on the patronage of families than did those resorts which still catered mainly for the elderly and infirm. In 1895 Llandudno became the first British seaside resort officially to reintroduce mixed bathing on part of its beach.[81] Other trendsetting resorts included Paignton in 1896, Cromer and Dawlish in 1897, Worthing and Bognor Regis in 1899, and Bridlington and Torquay in 1900.[82]

The case of Paignton illustrates how a seaside resort would reintroduce mixed bathing once it became convinced that otherwise it would lose trade. In the early summer of 1896, Paignton received several letters from prospective visitors enquiring if mixed bathing was permitted and warning that if it was not they would holiday at a

Plate 3. Bathing tents on the mixed-bathing section of the beach at Paignton, c.1902. Bathing machines were still in use in the segregated bathing areas. (Reproduced by kind permission of John Travis)

Plate 4. Gentlemen wearing neck-to-knee bathing costumes at Woolacombe, c.1907. Bathing tents would soon take the place of the bathing machines. (Reproduced by kind permission of Ilfracombe Museum)

Continental resort where it was allowed. One letter to the *Paignton Observer* asked:

> Why do we not adopt the Continental idea of mixed bathing? And why should not Paignton, with its unrivalled sands, be a pioneer in this matter? I feel confident that, were the experiment tried, many, who like myself now take their wives and families to French watering places, would flock to Paignton.[83]

The *Paignton Observer* also received another letter advocating mixed bathing which declared that the 'loin cloth' then worn by many male bathers was a 'disgusting' form of attire for those who wanted to bathe with ladies. The writer said that, if the sexes were to bathe together, he would 'judge any dress indecent which did not completely cover the body from the neck to the knees'.[84]

The Paignton tourist interest became increasingly concerned. This was a sandy-beach resort catering primarily for middle-class families, so any suggestion that some families might desert Paignton for Continental resorts had to be taken seriously. After several long debates the Paignton Urban District Council made an important decision. It resolved to allow the sexes to bathe together to the north of the pier (see Plate 3), although it played safe by keeping segregated bathing on the rest of the beach for those who might prefer it. The Council also insisted that all bathers in the mixed-bathing section should wear neck-to-knee costumes.[85] Business boomed following the reintroduction of mixed bathing.[86] Other South Devon seaside resorts found that Paignton was capturing some of their trade, so they were soon obliged to follow the example set by their progressive neighbour.[87]

In little more than a decade, mixed bathing became acceptable at almost all of the seaside resorts which had previously banned it. The English public were quick to demonstrate their approval. At resorts which offered both mixed and segregated bathing, happy holidaymakers packed the mixed-bathing areas, whereas only a few lonely bathers swam up and down in the segregated sections.

It was the resurgence of mixed bathing, rather than any new determination to enforce the by-laws, which eventually brought male nude bathing to an end. While seaside resorts had segregated bathing on at least part of their beaches, some males continued to bathe without a costume. However, male nude bathing was closely identified with the outdated idea of bathing for health, which was rapidly being superseded by the new concept of bathing for pleasure.

The old custom waned in popularity as fewer and fewer men believed that exposing their bare skin to the salt water actually improved their health. In the years leading up to the First World War, the last die-hards finally gave up the old custom of nude bathing so that they could enjoy the fun of bathing with members of the fair sex. Nude bathing had not been stamped out, it had survived until there was no longer a demand for it.

Everywhere on the English coast the introduction of mixed bathing presaged the eventual demise of the bathing machine, for, once bathers wore neck-to-knee costumes (see Plate 4) and the sexes were allowed to bathe together, there was no point in concealment before the water was reached. Bathing tents and bathing huts were less expensive to hire, and they cluttered the beach far less. Bathing machines were hauled out of the water for the last time and some were turned into beach huts. There they stood at the top of the beach, to be regarded as symbols of the rules and regulations of a bygone age. Their passing marked the end of an era.

Looking back over the nineteenth century it becomes clear that the sea-bathing issue was resolved to the satisfaction of commercial interests rather than moral reformers. Once it became apparent that many visitors preferred the old sea-bathing practices, the coastal resorts decided to swim with the tide rather than risk driving trade away by prosecuting those who infringed their by-laws.

So the history of English sea-bathing is one of continuity as well as change. The traditional sea-bathing practices had been assailed by powerful forces, but they had shown a remarkable ability to withstand sustained attack. Not until the very end of the nineteenth century had the old custom of male nude bathing begun to fall out of favour, and then only because the equally old custom of mixed bathing enjoyed a revival. As the twentieth century began, the English could look forward with optimism towards a new era of personal freedom, when there would be fewer attempts to regulate their behaviour while bathing in the sea.

NOTES

1   See, for example, A. Hern, *The Seaside Holiday: The History of the English Seaside Resort* (1967), 24, 34-5; J. Anderson and E. Swinglehurst, *The Victorian and Edwardian Seaside* (1978), 71-6.

2   There may have been an earlier tradition of poor people visiting the spas: J. Pimlott, *The Englishman's Holiday: A Social History* (Hassocks, 2nd edn, 1976), 25-6.

3   'Teignmouth', *The Royal Magazine*, VI (1762), 128. For a full account of the early development of the Devon seaside resorts see, J. Travis, *The Rise of the Devon Seaside Resorts, 1750-1900* (University of Exeter Press, 1993).

4   J.K. Walton, *The English Seaside Resort: A Social History, 1750-1914* (Leicester, 1983), 10.

5   Walton, *English Seaside Resort*, 10-11.

6   G. Williams, *History of the Liverpool Privateers and Letters of Marque with an Account of the Liverpool Slave Trade* (1966), 302. A reference by Cunningham led me to this book: H. Cunningham, 'Leisure and culture', in F.M.L. Thompson, ed., *The Cambridge Social History of Britain, 1750-1950* (Cambridge, 1990), II, 313.

7   J. Aiken, *A Description of the Country from Thirty to Forty Miles Round Manchester* (1795), quoted by E. Royston Pike, *Human Documents of Adam Smith's Time* (1974), 199.

8   R. Russell, *A Dissertation on the Use of Sea Water in the Diseases of the Glands* (1752), 68.

9   J.J. Cartwright, *The Travels through England of Dr Richard Pococke during 1750, 1751 and Later Years* (1888), I, 102.

10 A. Oliver, ed., *The Journal of Samuel Curwen, Loyalist* (Cambridge, Massachusetts, 1972), I, 547, 560.

11 P. Toynbee and L. Whibley, eds., *Correspondence of Thomas Gray* (1971), 851-2.

12 See, for example, H. Cunningham, *Leisure in the Industrial Revolution, c.1780-c.1880* (1980), 10-11, 36-8; P. Bailey, 'Custom, Capital and Culture in the Victorian Music Hall' in R.D. Storch, ed., *Popular Culture and Custom in Nineteenth Century England* (Oxford, 1982), 180-5; J. Hargreaves, *Sport, Power and Culture: A Social and Historical Analysis of Popular Sports in Britain* (Cambridge, 1986), 31, 39.

13 Samuel Jones, Gent., *Whitby: A Poem Occasioned by Mr Andrew Long's Recovery from the Jaundice, by Drinking of Whitby Spaw Waters* (1718), quoted by H.G. Stokes, *The Very First History of the English Seaside* (1947), 16. I am indebted to Bernard Hallen for this reference. For information about the poem and Whitby spa

see, F.K. Robinson, *Whitby, its Abbey and the Principal Parts of the Neighbourhood* (1860), 194-5. I am grateful to Enid Clarkson of Whitby Library for this reference.

14   *Universal Spectator*, 6 May 1832; *A Journey from London to Scarborough in Several Letters* (1734), 36. Bryan Berryman of Scarborough Library kindly provided the latter reference. Other early references to sea-bathing at Scarborough are to be found in *Scarborough Miscellany* (1732), 6-7; (1733), 10, 26-7; (1734), 16-18, 28-9. I am grateful to Andrew Farmer who looked up this reference, and others, for me at the British Library. It is likely that these bathers would have been dipping rather than swimming. Hardly any ladies could swim, those gentlemen who could swim used ponds and rivers rather than the sea; N. Orme, *Early British Swimming, 55 BC-AD 1719* (Exeter, 1983), 107.

15   J. Whyman, *The Early Kentish Seaside, 1736-1840: Kentish Sources VIII* (Gloucester, 1985), 160; Pimlott, *Englishman's Holiday*, 51-2. J.A. Barrett refers to sea-bathing at Bootle in 1721; J.A. Barrett, 'The Seaside Resorts of England and Wales' (unpublished PhD thesis, University of London, 1958), 6. I have been unable to track down the original source for the reference to bathing at Bootle so I have not been able to find out if the bathers were members of fashionable society or working people. I am grateful to John Whyman for the reference to Barrett's thesis and also for information about Margate.

16   Pimlott, *Englishman's Holiday*, 52.

17   Hern, *Seaside Holiday*, 66.

18   *Scarborough Miscellany* (1732), 6-7.

19   *Journey from London to Scarborough*, 36.

20   See for example T. Smollett, *The Expedition of Humphrey Clinker* (1771), 170; *An Historic and Descriptive Guide to Scarborough and Its Environs* (1787), 20.

21   Whyman, *Early Kentish Seaside*, 162, 182.

22   Whyman, *Early Kentish Seaside*, 182-3; Cartwright, *Travels through England*, II, 104.

23   J. Awsiter, *Thoughts on Brighthelmston, Concerning Sea-Bathing and Drinking Sea-Water* (1768), quoted in J.G. Bishop, *Brighton in the Olden Time* (1892), 227-8. I am indebted to Stephanie Green of Brighton Reference Library for this reference.

24   W. Hutton, *A Description of Blackpool in Lancashire, Frequented for Sea-bathing* (1789), 42.

25   R. Jones, ed., *John Skinner: West Country Tour: Diary of an Excursion through Somerset, Devon and Cornwall in 1797* (1985), 25.

26   Whyman, *Early Kentish Seaside*, 183.

27   *A Tour to Worthing* (1805), 72. I am indebted to Esme Evans of Worthing Library for information on Worthing.

28   P. Aughton, *North Meols and Southport: A History* (1989), 107. I am indebted to Danny and Simon Park who did research on Southport for me.

29   See, for example, *Observer*, 27 July, 30 Aug. 1857, 29 Aug. 1858, 28 Aug., 4 Sept. 1859; *Hastings and St Leonard's News*, 26 July 1850; *Llandudno Register*, 21, 28 July 1866. I am grateful to Justin and Emma Travis, my son and daughter, who helped me research at the Colindale Newspaper Library.

30   *Observer*, 16 July 1865.

31   R. Manning-Sanders, *Seaside England* (1951), 21.

32   *Observer*, 24 Aug. 1856.

33   *Observer*, 28 Aug. 1859.

34   *Western Times*, 21 Aug., 28 Aug., 4 Sept. 1858, 30 July, 27 Aug. 1859; *Exeter and Plymouth Gazette*, 28 Aug. 1858; Public Record Office (PRO), Rail, 631/5, South Devon Railway, 17 Aug. 1858. For a more detailed discussion see, Travis, *Rise of the Devon Seaside Resorts*, 120-1.

35   Cunningham, *Leisure in the Industrial Revolution*, 76.

36   *Scarborough Gazette*, 26 July 1866.

37   *Scarborough Gazette*, 9 Aug. 1866.

38   *Scarborough Mercury*, 8 Sept. 1866.

39   *Scarborough Mercury*, 16 Feb. 1867.

40   *Scarborough Gazette*, 9 Aug., 1 Nov. 1866, 16 Feb. 1867.

41   *Scarborough Gazette*, 1 Nov. 1866.

42   See, for example, *Bridlington Free Press*, 5 Aug., 12 Aug. 1871: cited in D. Cookson, *Seaside Resorts in Humberside* (Hull, 1987), 24.

43   PRO, MH 13/61, Local Government Act Office Correspondence with the Dawlish Local Board, 1859. For a full discussion see, Travis, *Rise of the Devon Seaside Resorts*, 180-1.

44   *Sidmouth Directory*, 1 Aug. 1863.

45   PRO, MH/12, Local Government Board Correspondence with the Seaton Local Board, 12 Jan. 1877.

46   Bishop, *Brighton in the Olden Time*, 237-8.

47   *Brighton Gazette*, 18 Aug. 1825.

48   *Observer*, 17 Sept. 1865.

49   At Scarborough, for example: *Scarborough Gazette*, 26 July 1866.

50   *Observer*, 10 Sept. 1865.

51   *Observer*, 24 Aug., 14 Sept. 1862.

52   F. Stafford and N. Yates, *The Later Kentish Seaside, 1840-1974: Kentish Sources, IX* (Gloucester, 1985), 41-2; *Thanet Advertiser*, 18 July 1863.

53 *Thanet Advertiser*, 18 July 1863.

54 *Observer*, 30 July 1865.

55 *Observer*, 16 Sept. 1866.

56 *Pall Mall Gazette*, 7 Sept. 1866.

57 *Observer*, 20 Aug., 10 Sept. 1865.

58 *Observer*, 16 July 1865.

59 *Scarborough Gazette*, 26 July 1866; *Scarborough Mercury*, 8 Sept. 1866; *Observer*, 16 Sept. 1866.

60 *Pall Mall Gazette*, 7 Sept. 1866.

61 J. H. Adams, 'Bathing at the English Seaside Resorts', *Cosmopolitan*, XIX (1895), 395-404. For reference to early morning nude bathing at Tenby see, *Tenby Observer*, 20 Aug. 1896; and for Teignmouth see, *Devon and Exeter Gazette*, 4 Aug. 1899.

62 A.R.H. Moncrieff, *Where Shall We Go?* (14th edn, 1899), 35-6, 96, 222; *Daily Telegraph*, 19, 25, 28 Aug. 1897; *Daily Mail*, 17 Aug. 1896; *Bognor Observer*, 29 July 1896.

63 Moncrieff, *Where?*, 96.

64 *Daily Graphic*, 10 Sept. 1895.

65 Pimlott, *Englishman's Holiday*, 129-30, 182.

66 See, for example, Swinglehurst, *Victorian and Edwardian Seaside*, 76; Manning-Sanders, *Seaside England*, 41; S. Everitt, *Southend Seaside Holiday* (Chichester, 1980), 36.

67 *Standard*, 15-16 June 1896; *Tenby Observer*, 25 June 1896; *Scarborough Post*, 21 Aug. 1896; *Barmouth Advertiser*, 3 Sept. 1896; *Daily Mail*, 17, 18, 21 Aug. 1896.

68 *Daily Graphic*, 2 Sept. 1895.

69 *Daily Graphic*, 31 Aug. 1895.

70 *Daily Mail*, 11 Aug. 1896.

71 *Daily Graphic*, 17 Aug.-16 Sept. 1895; *Standard*, 13, 15, 16 June 1896; *Daily Mail*, 4-28 Aug. 1896; *Daily Telegraph*, 17 Aug.-4 Sept. 1897.

72 *Daily Mail*, 15, 19, 20, 28 Aug. 1896; *East Kent Times*, 19 Aug. 1896. The wording of the petition is given in *Thanet Times*, 21 Aug. 1896.

73 See, for example, *Daily Graphic*, 29 Aug., 7 Sept. 1895; *Daily Mail*, 5, 15, 17, 18, 19 Aug. 1896.

74 See, for example, *Blackpool Herald*, 25 Aug. 1896; *Daily Mail*, 15 Aug. 1896.

75 *Daily Graphic*, 6 Sept. 1895.

76 Adams, 'Bathing', 395.

77 See, for example, *Truth*, 29 Aug. 1895; *Daily Graphic*, 23 Aug. 1895; *Scarborough Post*, 21 Aug. 1896.

78 *Standard*, 13 June 1896.

79   *Daily Graphic*, 17 Aug. 1895.

80   *Blackpool Herald*, 25 Aug. 1896.

81   *Daily Graphic*, 5 Sept. 1895.

82   *Paignton Observer*, 13 Aug. 1896; *Daily Telegraph*, 19 Aug. 1897; *Teignmouth Times*, 13 Aug. 1897; *Worthing Gazette*, 7 June 1899 (I am indebted to Esme Evans of Worthing Library for this latter reference); R. Iden, 'The Hazards of Sea-bathing in Victorian Bognor', *Bognor Regis Local History Society*, VII (1984), 30 (I am indebted to M.A. Hayes of Worthing Library for this reference); *Bridlington Free Press*, 20 July 1900 (I am indebted to the staff of the Bridlington Library for this reference); *Torquay Times*, 14 Sept., 5 Oct. 1900.

83   *Paignton Observer*, 11 June 1896.

84   *Paignton Observer*, 30 July 1896.

85   *Paignton Observer*, 23 July, 13 Aug. 1896.

86   *Paignton Observer*, 20 Aug. 1896.

87   Travis, *Rise of the Devon Seaside Resorts*, 182. Resorts in North Devon were slower to follow; Ilfracombe in 1906 and Lynmouth in 1907. For Lynmouth see, J. Travis, *An Illustrated History of Lynton and Lynmouth, 1770-1914* (Derby, 1995), 171-4.

THE SEASIDE RESORTS OF WESTERN EUROPE, 1750-1939

John K. Walton

The fashion for therapeutic and prophylactic sea-bathing under medical direction, or at least advice, was in the modern world an English invention. So was its rapid association with the organised and commercialised pursuit of pleasure as well as health, in the established manner of the eighteenth-century spa resorts. The first evidence of the capacity of this combination of health and enjoyment for transforming local maritime economies, and even for stimulating the growth of new towns, was also an English phenomenon, with the rise of Brighton, Margate and their marine rivals from the middle decades of the eighteenth century.

Over the ensuing two centuries sea-bathing and its associated pleasures (whatever their relationship with the sea itself) passed through many vicissitudes in England. Seaside resorts sprouted and ramified on every coastline, though they clustered and flourished more mightily in some areas than in others. The seaside holiday moved downmarket, as merchants and the more elevated professionals and manufacturers soon joined the aristocracy and gentry at the seaside, and the fashion trickled down thereafter to come within the reach of the lower middle and working classes during the nineteenth century. The most dynamic of the seaside resorts came to rank among the fastest-growing towns of the nineteenth century, in spite of the fierce competition provided by other kinds of town in that rapidly-urbanizing period. Sea-bathing resorts were joined as favourite places of rest and recuperation by places whose stock in trade might be scenery, pure air, and literary or historical associations; and some of these were also beside the sea, reminding us that the category 'seaside resort' is far from straightforward, and that many seaside towns continued to combine resort with other functions.

The pattern of seaside entertainment changed, especially in those resorts which became attractive to the working class of Victorian and subsequent years, although even in the age of 'mass entertainment' there remained something distinctive about the seaside's offerings at least until the inter-war years. And the role of the beach itself changed over time, as the careful regulations of bathing in the interests of modesty and decorum which reached its apogee in Victorian resorts gave way, gradually and piecemeal, in the twentieth century to a much freer and more tolerant regime. In addition, swimming and splashing for pleasure replaced the regimented medicinal bathe, and the fashion for sunbathing made its own distinctive contribution to the transformation of public behaviour on the shoreline. But these changes in the use made of that debatable land and border zone between land and sea, whose very ownership was for a long time in dispute in many resorts, were imported from more relaxed seaside regimes and more reliable climates on the Continent of Europe, rather than being indigenous to Britain; and this reminds us that sea-bathing, the seaside holiday and the seaside resort had been prominent in their time among British cultural exports in the eighteenth and nineteenth centuries.

The seaside holiday stands alongside Association Football as one of the most popular and ubiquitous cultural exports of this kind, although different European countries and cultures, and indeed those much further afield, have developed their own styles of enjoying beach and sea, just as they have created their own distinctive footballing idioms. Why the seaside and football should have proved so much more exportable than (for example) cricket and fish and chips opens out interesting questions, which lie beyond the scope of this paper. What follows is an initial analysis of the spread of sea-bathing and the seaside holiday in the Europe of the Industrial Revolution, over nearly two centuries between the mid-eighteenth century and the Second World War, and an attempt to chart the diffusion and development of the seaside resort as a distinctive kind of town.[1]

A European survey of seaside resort history is still a highly problematic task. As we shall see, sea-bathing and its associated activities spread from England into France, Germany and the Low Countries, then south into Spain, and later still into Italy and Portugal. The historiography of the seaside seems to be following a similar path. It is well-developed in England itself (but not in Scotland or Ireland, where sea-bathing resorts were comparatively much less important, while there is patchy and undeveloped coverage of the Welsh seaside). There are significant stirrings in France, with, for example, a pioneering study of changing attitudes to and perceptions of the sea in relation to the rise of sea-bathing and maritime tourism, a survey of resort development on the coast of Normandy, and a monumental work on the rise of Pau, Biarritz and the neighbouring French resorts.[2] There is also a considerable literature on the Côte d'Azur, which was in most respects a late developer as a sea-bathing rather than a climatic and cultural resort coastline.[3] Local historians with some academic pretensions have worked on Ostend and Scheveningen, meanwhile;[4] but the Germans have been slower to explore the histories of their coastal resorts (although there are probably local histories of individual resorts), and the most evocative way in to this territory probably remains Thomas Mann's *Buddenbrooks*.[5] Spanish regional and local researchers are quite active, however, although much of the work here is being done under the aegis of geography and town planning departments rather than through social and economic history, and this skewing of disciplinary interests obviously affects the agenda and output.[6] I know of no academic activity in seaside resort history in Italy or Portugal, or indeed Scandinavia; but a preliminary survey of this kind is bound to be affected in its coverage by the linguistic competences and academic contacts of the writer, and mine lean heavily towards France and Spain. Nevertheless, the current state of historians' interest in the European seaside is at much the same stage as the distribution of sea-bathing resorts in Europe about 1850, although the French interest in the phenomenon is apparently of independent origin, whereas the rise of their sea-bathing resorts in the first instance was directly influenced by the English. The introductory survey of sea-bathing and seaside resorts in Western Europe begins with the early developments on the Channel coast, and proceeds largely through the examination of guidebooks and contemporary surveys, helped out by the few secondary works to have appeared so far and by archival research on the resorts of Spain's Biscay coast, especially San Sebastián.[7]

The paper begins with a sketch of the pattern of seaside resort development across Europe from the first stirrings to the Second World War. The focus will be mainly but not exclusively on Western Europe, and the treatment will be broad and introductory. Some attempt will then be made to identify and explain the development of resort clusters or local networks in certain parts of Europe, and three case studies (one each in England, France and Spain) will be presented to illustrate and account for the disproportionate success (measured in terms of sustained population growth) of some resorts rather than others. Relatedly, the strength and direction of demand flows to seaside resorts in different parts of Western Europe will be discussed, again in a qualitative and introductory way, and the development of seaside resorts will be set in context alongside the enduring and emerging importance of other kinds of health and pleasure resort.

The current state of research is such that any overview of the pattern of seaside resort growth in Western Europe must necessarily be impressionistic. The collection of basic population statistics is still a thing of the future, and no overviews are available for visitor numbers: Ogilvie's pioneering review of European tourism, which was written in 1933, shows that despite the efforts which were being made in countries such as Italy by that time, no usable statistics of tourist numbers were pulled together in such a way that they could be disaggregated by type of holidaymaking or by individual resort.[8] It is clear that a lot of interesting work can be done at the level of individual resorts, however, and this seems to offer the best route forward in the long run. For San Sebastián, Spain's pioneer fashionable seaside resort (and easily its most dynamic and successful one before the Spanish Civil War), there are three ways of pursuing an understanding of trends in visitor numbers over time. There are returns of railway passenger arrivals, although these are not disaggregated as between holidaymakers or tourists and other kinds of passengers, and there are wild and unexplained fluctuations from one year to the next which suggest inconsistencies in collection and recording.[9] Secondly, there are municipal calculations of the numbers of passengers arriving at and departing from the railway stations during the summer, which were used to present day-by-day statistics on the number of visitors in the town, which were published in the local press. The problems posed by this procedure are obvious, especially as the counting was done by ill-paid railway workers and policemen who also had other responsibilities; and it is clear that by the end of the First World War the system was breaking down, leading to an inflation of the September figures which is not supported by other evidence.[10] Finally, there are the returns from the provincial entertainment tax which was levied on box-office receipts between 1915 and 1932, which may be regarded as a surrogate for the measurement of the holiday season month by month and year by year, although it includes the expenditure of locals as well as visitors and cannot readily be converted into a measure of visitor numbers.[11] Despite the difficulties which are evident in this unusually well-documented example, there is clearly plenty of scope for building up a composite picture of European seaside resort experiences from local studies, especially as studies based in France and Germany have shown that local listings of visitors and taxes on visitors and property provide opportunities for the analysis of the changing fortunes of individual resorts.[12] But this is largely an agenda for future research.

Meanwhile, an interim overview can help to influence the working out of that agenda. In what follows, the well-documented British experience will be taken as read, apart from the use of Brighton as a comparative case-study, and the dominant focus will be on the spread of sea-bathing and other seaside resorts on the European 'mainland'.[13] In a formal, organized way, in association with the recommendations of orthodox medicine and the growth of commercial trappings, the story begins in the late eighteenth century, and its first chronicler, in a very Gallic and rather Foucauldian style, is Alain Corbin.[14] But, as Corbin himself suggests in passing, there was (as in England) a pre-history of popular sea-bathing, which surfaces in various nineteenth-century sources at, for example, Biarritz, Santander and Oporto, usually in mid-August and with some relationship to a religious festival.[15] So the sea as something magically prophylactic and therapeutic which could be propitiated and harnessed to health through bathing rituals predates its capture by 'official' medicine in Europe as in Britain, suggesting that sea-bathing was a practice which spread upwards from popular culture before it percolated downwards again from high society.[16]

Corbin shows formal sea-bathing seasons emerging on the French Channel coast from the late eighteenth century onwards: half a century after the first similar stirrings in England, and responding in part to the influence of a developed network of seaside resorts in (especially) south-eastern England. English bathers, indeed, were in evidence at Boulogne – and further north at Ostend – during the respite between Anglo-French wars which lasted from 1783 to 1792. But it was not until the Restoration years after 1815, and most obviously in the 1820s, that sustained investment in sea-bathing seasons began. French aristocratic interest was in evidence, especially in the person of the Duchesse de Berry, who was an important influence on the rise of fashionable bathing seasons at Dieppe and, from 1828, Biarritz.[17] The other early stirrings of coastal tourism in France took place on what became the French Riviera, but at this stage Nice and its environs were emerging as winter climatic stations rather than sea-bathing resorts.[18] Corbin emphasizes that the French had been culturally prepared for sea-bathing by an artistic and literary revaluing of the sea and of marine landscapes, but it seems hard to avoid the conclusion that the growth of sea-bathing in France as an élite activity with commercial implications was kick-started by British seekers after cheapness, informality and the lure of 'abroad', just as the British were at the core of the early development of the Riviera.[19]

Sea-bathing also began early in some of the North German states, and little resorts began to proliferate in the 1790s, on the shores of both the North Sea and the Baltic. Here the British influence was at one remove, through the original impetus to development which came from a doctor who had spent time at Margate and took Deal as a model to emulate. But these places seem to have had regional and *bourgeois* visiting publics, although evidence on this is still limited. Thomas Mann's portrayal of resort life towards the mid-nineteenth century, in *Buddenbrooks*, seems to bear this picture out.[20] The German seaside resorts proved less competitive with the inland spas than did their French counterparts; but meanwhile, further west, Ostend began to grow in earnest after the Napoleonic Wars, when Scheveningen began its career as the leading Dutch sea-bathing resort.[21]

Spanish seaside resorts were also among the relatively early developers, perhaps surprisingly in the light of that country's poor transport system and the long distances from Madrid – the main concentration of moneyed demand – to the coast. Significantly, it was the Atlantic coast rather than the Mediterranean that took the lead, especially in the north on the Bay of Biscay. This reflected the spread from England via France of sea-bathing prescriptions which advocated cold, powerful seas and bracing climates, and the eagerness of people from central Spain to escape from the stifling heat and dust of the summer months. Members of the Spanish royal family were bathing at San Sebastián in 1830, under the influence of the ubiquitous Duchesse de Berry, and a bathing season was firmly established in the Basque resort by 1839.[22] Santander followed suit from the mid-1840s, with the tentative initial development of the bathing beaches of the Sardinero, and other sea-bathing places began to emerge along the same coastline.[23] There were also early stirrings on the Atlantic coast in south-western Spain at Sanlúcar de Barrameda, where the Duc de Montpensier had a seaside villa; but evidence for a possible emergence of a bathing season before 1830 is at best equivocal.[24] Meanwhile, on the Mediterranean coast Málaga was being tentatively recommended to intrepid English people as a winter climatic resort by the 1840s, as (in a very small way) was nearly Torremolinos; but this was, at this stage, a false dawn.[25]

These were the main foci of seaside resort development in Europe before the railway age. It should be emphasised that the Spanish and German bathing-places, like the British ones, were essentially catering for domestic demand, although the British were already mobilising more of it further down the social scale than elsewhere. It was only France that had (in any sense) international seaside resorts by the mid-century; but when international high society foregathered in pursuit of health and pleasure it was at the spa rather than the sea-bathing place.

It is not altogether surprising that the earliest survey of seaside resorts to come to light so far which displays pretensions to European coverage should be a French production, the *Album Universel des Bains de Mer* of 1864.[26] Nor is it surprising that it shows a strong bias in its

Recreation and the Sea

coverage towards French resorts, including a professed belief that sea-bathing was first introduced to polite society at Dieppe. Of this publication's seventy three seaside resort entries – despite its title, it listed many more spas – fifty five were French. Eleven were in the north on the Channel coast; as many as twenty one were in Normandy, reflecting a recent rise in the popularity of this area as railways began to make access from Paris easier; seven were in Brittany; ten in the south-west; and six on the Mediterranean, where sea-bathing in the summer was a matter mainly for the locals, and the aristocratic and plutocratic *hivernants* of Nice, Cannes and their emergent neighbours were part of a different world.[27] Outside France there were only eight British listings – perhaps one-tenth of the actual number – and they included (surprisingly) Dover and Guernsey as well as 'Brighthon' and 'Worthung'. Scarborough was the lone representative north of Margate, apart from a ninth entry Heligoland, which was at this time a British possession and was listed as being in 'Angleterre, comté de Sussex'. This apart, there were five German and two Belgian entries, but hints at the wider spread of the sea-bathing fashion were provided by isolated entries from Sweden and the Austro-Hungarian side of the Adriatic.

Over the next thirty years, as the spread of European railway systems – and steamboat services – eased travel, the choices for the aspiring and footloose sea-bather widened alarmingly. Most resorts remained regional in their catchment areas, however, although demand from capital cities spread its tentacles widely. Désert's study of the seaside resorts of Normandy shows the importance of the role of the railways and of Parisian demand on an important French coastline, supplementing a smaller-scale provincial market to stimulate the emergence of an early resort system.[28] Similarly the opening of rail links between Madrid and San Sebastián, and later Santander, also brought new resorts into being on the coastlines between and beyond the railheads even before narrow-gauge rail networks began to fill in the gaps in the late nineteenth century, as summer visitors showed an impressive tolerance of long journeys by diligence to reach destinations which were preferred for cheapness and tranquility.[29]

A useful snapshot of the state of seaside resort development in Europe towards the end of the nineteenth century is provided by B. Bradshaw's *Bathing Places and Climatic Health Resorts*, published in 1893. This was the fullest and most convincing of several publications of this sort at this time, which itself suggests a developing perception of the market possibilities in this field.[30] Bradshaw was not infallible: to describe Runcorn as a sea-bathing resort, in the sewage- and

42

chemical-contaminated upper Mersey estuary, was not merely perverse but positively dangerous, while the inclusion of Shap, high among the Westmorland fells, in the list of seaside resorts is (if possible) even odder. Among the 427 sea-bathing places in this guide (it is worth noting that they were outnumbered by inland spas and other kinds of resort) were 205 in the British Isles; but a full country-by-country list of the European resorts in Bradshaw is well worth perusal.

Table 1

Distribution by Country of European Seaside Resorts Listed in B. Bradshaw's *Bathing Places and Climatic Health Resorts* (1893)

British Isles 205 (England 127, Wales 30, Ireland 24, Scotland 20, Isle of Man 2, Channel Islands 2)

France	96	Portugal	4
Germany	40	Sweden	4
Spain	29	Austria-Hungary	3
Italy	26	Denmark	2
Holland	6	Greece	1
Russia (including		Malta	1
Estonia and Finland)	5	Norway	1
Belgium	4		

This list includes Runcorn but excludes Shap. Bradshaw also included three sea-bathing resorts in the United States of America, two in Egypt and one in Algeria, but these were merely token representatives of the wider world.

A lot of these resorts were very small, but the overall pattern of development is probably pretty accurate. Continuing English dominance was genuine and not a product of the London location of the compilers of the list. England not only had far more seaside resorts than other European countries; it also had an unparalleled array of substantial towns in this category, with heavy investment in sea defences, piers, promenades and entertainments. There was nothing elsewhere in Europe to match the burgeoning lower middle-class and working-class demand which was already evident in parts of England, although Arcachon was near enough to Bordeaux to attract Sunday day-trippers, Santander was visited by modestly-off farming families from the Castilian wheatlands, and some of the winter resorts of the Italian Riviera were visited by plebeian sea-bathers from Genoa in the summer months.[31] Even elsewhere in

Britain seaside resorts were of very limited dimensions, with some exceptions in Wales, most obviously along the north coast. France had well-developed resort systems on several coastlines by this time, but away from the most direct influences of English and Parisian demand in the north, and apart from the very special case of the Riviera, even the most fashionable international resorts, like Deauville/Trouville and Biarritz, were much smaller than their English counterparts.

France had, nevertheless, the most developed seaside resort network on the European mainland, although Belgium's short coastline, which featured Ostend as a rapidly-growing international resort, was pulling its full weight.[32] San Sebastián, and Santander's seaside suburb of El Sardinero, stood out as Spain's only really substantial seaside resort towns, and Bradshaw's list includes several very small places on the Biscay coast (although not all of the possible ones), including Ondárroa which is described helpfully as being '42 miles from Zumárraga' and whose main distinguishing feature was held to be its amazing cheapness. There was also some demonstrable bias in Bradshaw's geographical coverage in Spain, which left out several well-frequented places in the south, such as Sanlúcar de Barrameda.[33] No large centre at all can be identified among the German sea-bathing resorts, which were still dwarfed by the larger spas, among which Wiesbaden stands out as one of the great European leisure towns. In Western Europe the most obvious gap in the seaside resort map was the Spanish Mediterranean, although Portugal was also a relatively late developer. Further east stirrings were just beginning on the Dalmatian coast, but the only Greek entry on the list was Corfu, which had (significantly) been a British possession since 1864. The very limited number of seaside resorts listed east of Italy and Germany almost certainly reflects a genuine lack of development, because coverage of spa resorts in Austria-Hungary, Russia, Greece and even Turkey was thorough and convincing.[34]

Between the early 1890s and the First World War these existing patterns were largely reinforced. In France, the rise of Brittany alongside Normandy as a provider of seaside resorts of differing sizes, price structures and social tones for Parisians, Britons and French bourgeois provincials, which was already in evidence by the 1880s, continued impressively, while in northern France and Belgium chains of small resorts were joined to the main centres by tramways and light railways, and the Belgian coast began to be systematically developed by land companies which established planned settlements among the sand-dunes.[35] Spain's seaside resort network extended westwards along the Atlantic coast to Gijón, La Coruña and Galicia in the wake of railway extensions, but the Mediterranean still languished from a sea-bathing point of view, apart from beaches in and on the outskirts of the big cities.[36] The Portuguese coast came into the reckoning, competing for Spanish demand in the early twentieth century, through a combination of cheap rail fares and resort prices. Within this framework Estoril emerged as an international resort on the 'Portuguese Riviera', at a time when 'rivieras' were sprouting all over Europe, from Cornwall to the Baltic.[37] Italian seaside resorts continued to expand and proliferate, and the Dalmatian coast saw accelerated seaside resort development, with Abbazia (Opatija) calling itself 'the Nice of the Adriatic'. German demand was important in both these areas.[38] An international guide of 1907 also referred to Constanza as a Rumanian seaside resort, while in Bulgaria the Black Sea coast around Varna was attracting bathers. So the seaside habit was spreading further across Europe and beginning to colonise coastlines in the distant east by the First World War, including Odessa on the Crimean peninsula, where sea-bathing supplemented the therapeutic offerings of the radioactive mud baths.[39]

The First World War damaged the seaside holiday industry in some parts of Europe, with the Belgian coast the most obvious sufferer; but on the other hand San Sebastián, in neutral Spain, did well out of the war, as did many resorts in England which benefited from the training and convalescence needs of the armed forces and the enhanced spending power of industrial workers. In any event, it offered only a brief interruption to established trends. In much of Western Europe the growing use of the motor-car and motor-bus gave a further stimulus to the proliferation of small resorts outside the major centres, although this did not prevent the larger resorts from continuing to flourish in a period when expanding demand defied economic fluctuations and difficulties. Previously undeveloped coastlines continued to make up for lost time, as in Portugal and the eastern Baltic (Poland and the new republics) as well as what was now Yugoslavia.[40] The intriguing exception continued to be Spain's Mediterranean coast, even as the French Riviera developed its summer sea- and sun-bathing season for the rich from the late 1920s.[41] The Italian Riviera had long catered for sea-bathing locals, and increasingly for Germans, when the English winter visitors had gone. So it does seem surprising that the potential Spanish Riviera – which was often so described in the early twentieth century – showed such limited stirrings in the summers of the 1920s and 1930s. There was very little activity on the Costa Brava before the Spanish Civil War, although places like Lloret, Sitges and even Salou had small visiting seasons. Mallorca was beginning to attract a moneyed and bohemian international public by the 1930s, but development was limited by a slow and unattractive steamer service. Further south, there were small beginnings but no more, apart from the established local beach resorts near Valencia and Alicante and the winter climatic season at Málaga. There was sea-bathing on a limited scale at Algeciras (stimulated partly by English demand from Gibraltar) and Torremolinos by the 1930s, and attempts were being made to promote Motril; but development was conspicuous by its limitations. Transport was part of the problem, given the lack of a coastal railway; but the road-building obsession of the Primo de Rivera dictatorship between 1923 and 1930 offered a potential for development which was not yet being realised. But above all, what counted was the lack of indigenous demand: Spaniards preferred the relatively cool and bracing Northern coast and the Atlantic rollers, which were still being prescribed by doctors, while they also preferred the built environment and *ambience* of San Sebastián and its neighbours. This made it more difficult to stimulate resort growth on new coastlines, and the Spanish Mediterranean continued to drowse until the age of the long-distance coach, the airborne package holiday and foreign visitors from northern Europe.[42]

Elsewhere in Europe, however, there were by the 1930s several clearly-defined seaside resort clusters or holiday regions, which increasingly offered complementary attractions to more mobile visitors. The most complex and heavily-populated were in England and Wales, and had already emerged by the later nineteenth century: the Sussex coast, the Fylde coast of Lancashire on either side of Blackpool, the Kent coast around Margate and Ramsgate, the North Wales coast and the Essex coast around Southend were the most prominent examples.[43] On the European mainland the most spectacular case was the French Riviera, which was a maverick example because its origins lay in its winter climate, and sea-bathing only came into the equation seriously in the inter-war years. In effect, this particular phenomenon was no respecter of national boundaries, for it extended into Italy to Genoa and beyond, although the main centres of fashion continued to lie in the area of Nice, Cannes and Monte Carlo.[44] British demand was enduringly important here, as it was on the Channel coast, where again the well-articulated resort cluster of northern France crossed the border into Belgium, whose resorts developed apace in the inter-war years. Normandy and Brittany had well-established resort clusters of their own, connected by transport systems along the coast and catering for a variety of tastes, by the early twentieth century; and further south another transnational cluster brought together the Basque resorts on either side of the Franco-Spanish frontier, from Biarritz to Zarauz and on to Zumaya and Deva, with San Sebastián at the core. There were plenty of strings of resorts across miles of coastline in other areas, but as in north Germany, Poland and the Baltic states, the scale seems to have been much smaller. But all this paragraph can do at this stage is to point to the possibilities for further research.

Within this framework, many of whose details remain flimsy and provisional, it may be useful to pursue the better-documented and more successful of Europe's seaside resorts over the period, enquiring into the distinctive characteristics which boosted and sustained their growth. The resorts selected for this exercise were the largest and, in the long run, the fastest growing in population terms, of the specialised seaside resorts in their respective countries: Brighton in England, Nice in France, and San Sebastián in Spain. Table 2 presents their population growth records on the basis of censuses taken out of season between about 1840 and the 1930s.

Table 2
Comparative Population Figures (off-season) for the Largest Seaside Resorts in Britain, France and Spain

Brighton		Nice		San Sebastián	
1841	46,000	1838	33,811	1840s	10,000
1861	77,000	1861	48,273	1860	14,111
1881	107,546	1881	66,000	1877	21,355
1911	131,237	1911	143,000	1910	49,008
1931	147,427	1936	241,926	1930	78,432

Source: National Census Returns for the three countries.

Some initial comments should be made on this table. Brighton's figures do not include the adjoining resort and residential town of Hove, which jealously guarded its separate identity for local government and therefore census purposes. It had a population of 20,804 in 1881, 42,173 in 1911 and 54,993 in 1931. The 'Brighton conurbation', as defined by the geographer E.W. Gilbert, embraced several other adjoining coastal settlements and contained 189,909 inhabitants in 1911 and 226,857 in 1931.[45] Nice was also at the centre of a chain of resorts, but it lacked the conurbation characteristics ascribed to Brighton by Gilbert; so it could be argued that it was not until the 1920s (the birth of the international summer season on the

French Riviera) that Nice overtook Brighton.[46] Meanwhile, San Sebastián had a small 'conurbation' of its own in the form of the adjoining small industrial town of Rentería and, beyond that, the port of Pasajes; but these were economically much more distinct in their functions and the scale was anyway significantly different.

Off-season population is, of course, not the only possible measure of 'success', and the pursuit of more satisfactory indicators must be one of the future preoccupations of seaside resort historians. In growing beyond a certain size resorts run the risk of losing some of their original attractiveness, and 'success' in growth terms may ultimately require a diversification away from or even beyond the original resort function.[47] An alternative way of conceptualising a successful *resort* might lie in the relationship between resident population and those who service them.[48] On this model really successful resorts, as such, would be places like Deauville/Trouville or Biarritz, with highly fashionable visiting publics and (especially in the case of Biarritz) multiple visiting seasons, but displaying only modest growth in their resident populations. For the time being, though, the very magnitude of these towns' growth on a seaside resort foundation in the context of their respective national economies and patterns of urban growth makes them worthy of comparative study.

The first point to emphasize is that each of the three resorts took a significantly different path to sustained growth. Brighton, one of the first substantial English sea-bathing resorts, had a great early boost from royal patronage, as it became the favoured resort of the Prince of Wales, later the Prince Regent and King George IV, from the late eighteenth century. The impetus from this auspicious beginning drove Brighton to its remarkable size as a specialised seaside resort by the dawn of the railway age in 1841, and this in turn helped to ensure early rail communication with London, which was a vital asset in the uniquely and increasingly competitive circumstances of the seaside holiday market in England. Even at this stage, however, Brighton was flexible and open to new influences: it made an early switch from a late autumn to a summer-dominated season, and managed to go downmarket by opening out to burgeoning middle-class demand while still retaining an aristocratic image and reputation. Brighton also moved, quite early in Victorian times if not earlier, from a predominant sea-bathing rationale to a basis in leisure, luxury and entertainment. The beach became less and less important in Victorian times, while the town found room for an extensive manufacturing base and was subsequently early in embracing seaside retirement and commuter populations. It is probable that this diversification of functions was mainly responsible for the town's continuing (but less dynamic) growth in the twentieth century.[49]

Nice was a larger town than Brighton before the advent of its visiting industry, and it prospered by catering for international high society rather than (as in Brighton's case) that of England (and especially London), although British visitors were enduringly important to its economy. Indeed, it owed its origins as a resort to English demand, but as it developed in the middle decades of the nineteenth century, and especially after the arrival of the railway in 1864, Paris became increasingly important to it. The relative earliness of the rail connection, bearing in mind the remoteness of the location and the difficulty of the terrain, owed something to the town's existing size and significance. By this time, however, and increasingly thereafter, Nice was becoming cosmopolitan in a way that British resorts have never been able to match, dependent as they remained to an overwhelming extent on home demand. Nice concentrated European demand for warmth, climatic comfort, health and high fashion, and its success in image creation was helped by the late Victorian rise of Monte Carlo and its enjoyably infamous casino within easy reach. Where Brighton's coastal neighbours were staid, respectable Worthing and Eastbourne, Nice's were Cannes and Monte Carlo. In the new century Nice was able to sustain its remarkably rapid growth (especially by French standards) by attracting the new sunbathing cult of high society in the 1920s, by not letting the elderly rich dominate its promenades and holiday enjoyments, and by becoming, unobtrusively, a retirement goal for the French middle classes. Nice, moreover, retained its royal patronage, but it came promiscuously from all over Europe and mingled excitingly with the new wealth of the Americas and indeed the super-rich of other continents.[50]

San Sebastián, by contrast, was faithful to the Spanish royal family, especially during the years between 1887 and 1928 when María Cristina, first Queen Regent, then Queen Mother, returned summer after summer, building a modest palace on the shore for her annual visit. Under these auspices San Sebastián became the summer seat of government – a feat that Brighton had never really matched – and this aspect of its identity was important enough for the town's governors to welcome the Republic with alacrity when the change of regime came in 1931, two years after the death of María Cristina. San Sebastián exploited a distinctive climatic reputation, offering seasonal escape from Madrid's suffocating summer heat, and it depended mainly on domestic demand, extending its appeal right across the Spanish provinces in the early decades of the twentieth century. It also had an international casino and sporting culture, especially during the First World War, and high society crossed the border from Biarritz for short visits; but San Sebastián was distinctive among the three resorts by depending largely on a *national* visiting public (Brighton's appeal was more to Londoners and the southern half of England). Its railway arrived early because it was strategically placed rather than already important, but like its English and French counterparts it adjusted well to widening its market, although it never succeeded in developing a winter season and continued to depend heavily on three lucrative months in the summer. What stands out is how dominant San Sebastián became in Spain's seaside holiday market, restricted as demand was by tardy and expensive transport and (above all and enduringly) by comparatively low and ill-distributed incomes. These limitations help to explain its smaller size compared with Brighton and Nice; but within the Spanish context its growth was really impressive.[51]

The obvious keynotes in common between the three resorts are threefold. First, the formative and persisting importance of royal patronage of one sort or another stands out; and this was a recurring theme across Europe, from Ostend to Abbazia, although fortunately for French resorts after 1870 imported royal patronage was as valuable as the home-grown sort. Secondly, resorts needed to be adaptable to changing market conditions and opportunities if they were to sustain their growth in the long run; they could not afford to allow themselves to become dominated by restrictive interest-groups which might erect barriers to new initiatives, but they also needed to be able to control development so as to protect the attractive and tranquil settings which were central to their appeal. This leads on to the third shared theme: the importance of local government. This was crucial to the creation and sustaining of an appropriate built environment, an attractive entertainment programme and a sense of peace, security and relaxation for visitors and wealthy residents; a sense that their lives, property and comfort were being looked after. Nowhere was private enterprise able to deliver this combination of essentials and combine it with sustained growth; not even in Blackpool, where the growth of the working-class market made this most plausible.[52] Large landed estates might go a long way towards delivering the goods, in England especially, and so might land companies; but they too eventually had to hand over power and responsibilities to representative bodies.[53] Among the three resorts in question here, Brighton and Nice perhaps had a more equal partnership between local government and a broadly consensual but not conflict-free private enterprise than did San Sebastián, where the municipality always had the outstanding role, with a particularly strong influence on planning and public order. Municipal government in enduringly successful resorts was able to articulate a shared sense of identity and mission which enabled towns to remake their images and recast their attractions to meet changing circumstances with a minimum of strife, although of course conflicts of interest were never absent. The role of municipal government, above all, merits further research and discussion.[54]

Natural advantages have not featured in this presentation of the distinguishing attributes of successful resorts, but we should not ignore them, although they were not distinctive enough to determine the fate of individual towns. Their nature was different in each case. Brighton's crucial advantage was its proximity to London, for neither its beach, nor its surroundings, nor its built environment were particularly attractive. Nice stood out for its climatic reputation, although in comparative terms this was above all a matter of medical perception and recommendation. San Sebastián flourished partly on the basis of a very different climatic reputation, but one which it shared with a broad tract of Atlantic coastline, and within this framework the peculiar delights of its beach and surrounding scenery should not be neglected. Indeed, San Sebastián was the only resort of the three where the beach remained central to its appeal, and the fierceness of the disputes over its regulation during the 1920s and 1930s bore witness to this, as the advent of sun bathing brought particular controversy.[55] Generally an essential aspect of the rolling process of renewal in successful seaside resorts was a gradual downgrading of the importance of natural as against artificial attractions, although this is a somewhat simplistic dichotomy and the changes were necessarily relative rather than absolute.

San Sebastián's advantages were such that it would have flourished more mightily on the cosmopolitan stage had it been more accessible to the two main streams of holidaymakers with a propensity for crossing frontiers and travelling long distances to favoured places: the British and the Germans. The British went everywhere, and were already becoming resident in their hundreds and even thousands in certain favoured Normandy and Brittany coastal resorts as well as in Boulogne by the late part of the nineteenth century.[56] The Germans, meanwhile, were already heading south to the Adriatic and the Italian Riviera, as well as westwards into France and Belgium; and this is certainly part of the reason for the slow growth of their own northern seaside resorts. Where British and Germans met, tensions were already in evidence and lasting stereotypes were being created. Here is Eustace A. Reynolds-Ball, writing in 1904 about the Italian or Levantine Riviera around Nervi:

> So marked indeed is the Teutonic immigration that English visitors are not likely to affect these resorts in any considerable numbers. Indeed, the Teutonic influence obtrudes itself unpleasantly at the hotel table d'hôte, sausages and an Italian form of sauerkraut being staple dishes, while your next neighbour is pretty certain to be a fat man in spectacles with his tucked-in serviette where his neck ought to be, and a foaming beaker of lager beer at his elbow.[57]

And here is Spencer C. Musson at Dinard in 1912: 'All nations and races seem represented in the motley throng: stalwart Germans claiming a place in the sun, and taking care to get it.'[58]

The early signs of tensions and stereotypes of this kind is only one of many strong themes for further research which emerge from this introductory overview of the development of European seaside resorts. The mixing of variegated visitor flows with different host populations in a framework of commercial exploitation opens out a rich agenda, over and above the need to trace the origins and growth of such an important international phenomenon as the tourist industry. Here, of course, we need to remember that the seaside resort, important as it became, was only one among many kinds of outlet, and the study of the seaside will need to be slotted in alongside, and examined in relation to, the development of other tourisms and leisure towns, involving spas, scenery, winter sports, cultural tourism and the exuberant proliferation of more recent novelties and subspecies. But the issues called forth by the study of the seaside resort in itself, as a kind of town and arena for contesting cultures and classes, and as a locus for the continuing struggle for dominance between humanity and nature on the liminal and evocative terrain of the seashore, offer an enticing field for further comparative research. This tentative introductory paper offers a provisional scheme for marking out the playing surface.

NOTES

1   For a survey of these issues in the context of England and Wales see, J.K. Walton, *The English Seaside Resort: a Social History, 1750-1914* (Leicester, 1983).

2   A. Corbin, *Le Territoire du Vide* (Paris, 1988); G. Désert, *La Vie Quotidienne sur les Plages Normandes du Second Empire aux Années Folles* (Paris, 1983); M. Chadefaud, *Aux Origines du Tourisme dans les Pays de l'Adour* (Pau, 1987). Corbin's book is now available in English as *The Lure of the Sea* (Cambridge, 1992).

3   C. James Haug, *Leisure and Urbanism in Nineteenth-century Nice* (Lawrence, Kansas, 1982); Mary Blume, *Côte d'Azur: Inventing the French Riviera* (London, 1992); Patrick Howarth, *When the Riviera was Ours* (London, 1977); V. Paschetta *Riviera/Côte d'Azur* (2nd edn., Nice, 1957).

4   Marc Constandt, *Een Eeuw Vakantie: 100 Jaar Toerisme in West-Vlaanderen* (Tielt, 1986); M. Nooren and A. Jansen, *Scheveningen Rond Kerk en Kurhaus* (Weesp, 1983).

5   Thomas Mann, *Buddenbrooks* (London, 1957 edn.).

6   A. Valero, 'El turismo de playa en España entre 1850 y 1950', *in Casa de Velázquez* (Madrid, 1991), 5-16; C. Gil de Arriba, *Casas Para Baños de Ola y Balnearios Marítimos en el Litoral Montañés, 1868-1939* (Santander, 1992).

7   J.K. Walton and J. Smith, 'The rhetoric of community and the business of pleasure: the San Sebastián waiters' strike of 1920', *International Review of Social History*, 39 (1994), 1-31; idem, 'The first century of beach tourism in Spain: San Sebastián and the "playas del norte", from the 1830s to the 1930s', in M. Barke, J. Towner, eds, *Tourism in Spain: Critical Perspectives* (Wallingford, 1995), 35-61.

8   F.W. Ogilvie, *The Tourist Movement* (London, 1945).

9   A. Valero, 'Chemin de fer et tourisme: l'exemple de Norte Principal (1877-1930)', *Mélanges de la Casa de Velazquez*, 27 (1991), 6-45, presents this material.

10 Walton and Smith, 'Beach tourism'.

11 *Ibid.*, using evidence from the 'Impuesto sobre espectáculos' files in Archivo General de Gipuzkoa, Tolosa.

12 Désert, *Plages Normandes*; J. Bennett-Ruete, 'The social history of Bad Ems', unpublished PhD thesis, Warwick University, 1987. An idiosyncratic recent comparative study is, J.V.N. Soane, *Fashionable Resort Regions* (Wallingford, 1993).

13 Walton, *Seaside Resort*, provides comparative background on England and Wales.

14   Corbin, *Territoire du Vide*. It should be noted that Corbin purports to discuss English developments in passing, but with no reference to any work published since the early 1950s.

15   This is documented in J.K. Walton, 'The world's first working-class seaside resort? Blackpool revisited, 1840-1974', *Transactions of the Lancashire and Cheshire Antiquarian Society*, 88 (1992), 1-30.

16   Compare, for example, Keith Chandler, *Ribbons, Bells and Squeaking Fiddles: a Social History of Morris-Dancing in the South Midlands*, Vol. 1 (London, 1993). See also, the paper by John Travis in this present volume.

17   Corbin, *Territoire du Vide*, chap. 5. Biarritz had been attracting bathers from Bayonne and district since the late eighteenth century, Chadefaud, *Aux Origines*.

18   J. Pemble, *The Mediterranean Passion* (Oxford, 1987), is good on this.

19   Haug, *Leisure and Urbanism*, 5-17; Corbin, *Territoire du Vide*, chap. 5.

20   Corbin, *Territoire du Vide*, chap.5.

21   Constandt, *Vakantie*; Nooren and Jansen, *Scheveningen*. This appears to be the most scholarly of several books on Scheveningen.

22   Valero, 'Turismo de playa'.

23   Walton and Smith, 'Beach tourism'.

24   Valero, 'Turismo de playa'.

25   Richard Ford, *A Hand-book for Travellers in Spain* (2nd edn., London, 1847), 116-17.

26   *Album Universel des Eaux Minérales, des Bains de Mer et des Stations d'Hiver; Troisième Année* (Paris, 1864).

27   Haug, *Leisure and Urbanism*, 47-8.

28   Désert, *Plages Normandes*.

29   Walton and Smith, 'Beach tourism'.

30   Two rival publications in the same year were Thomas Linn, *The Health Resorts of Europe* (London, 1893), and A.R.H. Moncrieff, *Where to Go Abroad* (London, 1893).

31   Walton, *Seaside Resort*, 24-39; Moncrieff, *Where to Go*, 313-15; J.M. de Pereda, *Tipos Trashumantes* (Santander, 1983 edn.), 23-32; Linn, *Health Resorts*, 271, 277.

32   J. Burney Yeo, *Climate and Health Resorts* (London, 1890 edn.), 132-3.

33   Walton and Smith, 'Beach tourism'.

34   B. Bradshaw, *Bathing Places and Climatic Health Resorts* (London, 1893), 393-409. Soane, *Fashionable Resort Regions*, has a short chapter on Wiesbaden.

35 Rosa Baughan, *The Northern Watering-Places of France* (London, 1886); Désert, *Plages Normandes*; George W.T. Omond, *Belgium* (London, 1928 edn.), 81-96.
36 Walton and Smith, 'Beach tourism'.
37 *The 'Queen' Newspaper Book of Travel* (London, 1907 edn.), 249.
38 Eustace A. Reynolds-Ball, *Mediterranean Winter Resorts* (London, 1904 edn.), 172-86, and advertisement for the Grand Hotel Stephanie, Abbazia.
39 Sir Hermann Weber and F. Parkes Weber, *Climatotherapy and Balneotherapy* (London, 1907 edn.), 100, 231.
40 E. Rosenthal, *Peeps at Portugal: a Pocket Guide to the 'Sun Coast' and Lisbon* (London, c.1930); M. Orlowicz, *Poland: North-Western Part, Illustrated Railway Guide* (Warsaw, 1932), 168-88, 223-8; Thomas Cook Archives, *Baltic Review, 1935*; E. Fodor, ed., *1938 in Europe* (London, 1938), 1303-13 (for Yugoslavia: there are interesting descriptions of seaside resorts in other countries as well).
41 Blum, *Côte d'Azur*, chaps 4-5.
42 F. Pérez García, *La Costa del Sol* (Motril, 1931); R. Elston, *Cook's Traveller's Handbook to Spain and Portugal* (London, 1930); C.L. Freeston, *The Roads of Spain* (London, 1930), chaps 14-18; H. Hessell Tiltman, *European Excursions* (London, 1936), chap. 6; Nancy J. Johnstone, *Hotel in Spain* (London, 1938); Lady Sheppard, *Mediterranean Island* (London, n.d.), for Mallorca.
43 Walton, *Seaside Resort*, chap. 3.
44 Blume, *Côte d'Azur*.
45 E.W. Gilbert, *Brighton. Old Ocean's Bauble* (Hassocks, 1975 edn.), 209-12.
46 Paschetta, *Riviera*, 19-22, 35-7.
47 Philip Cooke, ed., *Localities* (London, 1989), chap. 3, illustrates this point well for Cheltenham. See also comments and references in J.K. Walton, 'The remaking of a popular resort: Blackpool Tower and the booms of the 1890s', *Local Historian*, 24 (1994), 194-205.
48 J.K. Walton and P.R. McGloin, 'The tourist trade in Victorian Lakeland', *Northern History*, 17 (1981), 153-82.
49 See especially, Gilbert, *Brighton*, and C. Musgrave, *Life in Brighton* (London, 1970).
50 Haug, *Leisure and Urbanism*; Blume, *Côte d'Azur*; Paschetta, *Riviera*.
51 J.K. Walton and J. Smith, 'The first Spanish seaside resorts: San Sebastián and Santander from the 1840s to the 1930s', *History Today*, 44 (8) (August 1994), 23-9; Walton and Smith, 'San

Sebastián waiters' strike'; Walton and Smith, 'Beach tourism'. For Spain's estimated relative wealth in terms of per capita income, N.F.R. Crafts, *British Economic Growth during the Industrial Revolution* (Oxford, 1985), 57-9.

52 Walton, *Seaside Resort*, chaps 5-6.

53 D. Cannadine, *Lords and Landlords* (Leicester, 1980), Part III.

54 J.K. Walton and J. Walvin, eds, *Leisure in Britain, 1780-1939* (Manchester, 1983), chaps 8-10.

55 This is a sustained theme in the local press from the mid-1920s.

56 P. Gerbod, 'Voyageurs et residents britanniques en France au XIX siècle', *Acta Geographica*, December 1988, 19-24; Douglas Sladen, *Brittany for Britons* (London, 1896), 3; S. Pakenham, *60 Miles from England: the English at Dieppe, 1814-1914* (London, 1967).

57 Reynolds-Ball, *Mediterranean*, 174.

58 Spencer C. Musson, *La Côte d'Emeraude* (London, 1912), 43.

COASTAL TOURISM IN CORNWALL SINCE 1900

Paul Thornton

Introduction

Throughout its history the Cornish holiday industry, while experiencing mixed fortunes, has shown the ability significantly to influence both the economy and the local communities of Cornwall. In the early 1990s the county regularly attracted over three million tourists a year, who, in 1993, spent approximately £585 million on their holidays.[1] The social impact has also been considerable: at the peak of the 1991 summer season while there were 473,000 local residents there were also an estimated 250,000 visitors in Cornwall on any one day.[2]

This paper offers a brief overview of the development of the coastal tourism industry in Cornwall, and examines some of the prime factors that have controlled that development. In doing this, reference will be made to Butler's resort cycle model (see Figure 1).

Butler's model visualises the development of a destination area as an evolutionary cycle, consisting of several life-stages. The actual cyclical model is based upon the 'product life-cycle', where tourism is viewed as the product, and visitor numbers considered a substitute for sales. From this basis Butler sees the model as a means to explain the evolution and potential decay of tourist destination areas over a long period of time.[3]

The tourism cycle of evolution consists of six sequential stages, as shown in Figure 1. The first stage is described as involving 'Exploration', and is characterised by small numbers of visitors arriving in an area that provides few tourism facilities. This destination quickly proceeds into the 'Involvement' stage – where the local community responds by providing some basic facilities. At the same time factors such as increased advertising result in a seasonal variation in tourist numbers. Following on from this is the 'Development' stage, which is characterised by several traits. First, there is a rapid take-off in visitor numbers, with some identifiable changes in the nature of the tourists.[4] This normally consists of a change away from adventurous, independent travellers to those

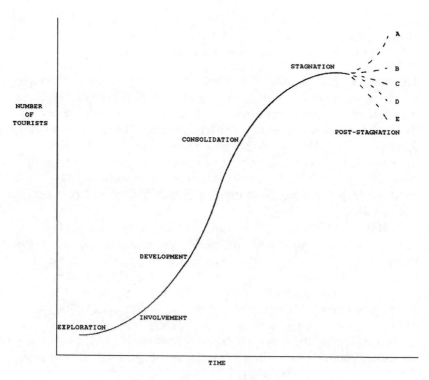

Figure 1. Butler's Resort Cycle Model.
Source: see footnote 3.

Select Seaside Tourist Towns of Cornwall

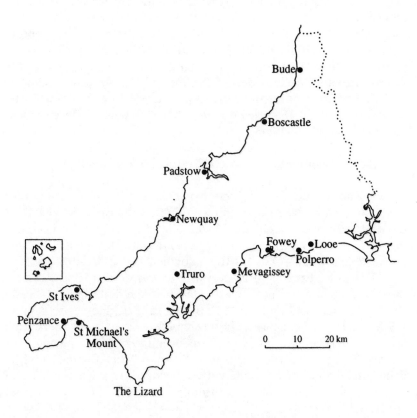

content to be in the company of other tourists. Secondly, the destination area develops additional tourist facilities and places greater effort into promotion. At the same time, it is argued, greater control of the tourist trade is assumed by outsiders, while increasing visitor numbers encourages antagonism between the host and guest populations.

By the 'Consolidation' stage, tourism has become a major element in the local economy. However, the growth rate in visitor numbers has begun to level off. Replacing the Consolidation stage is 'Stagnation' – during which visitor numbers peak as capacity levels are reached. Although the resort has a well established image, it is no longer in fashion as a destination. Within the resort the rapid establishment and failure of businesses results in high property turnover rates.[5] The end of the resort cycle is the Post-Stagnation phase, which consists of five possibilities – namely, Rejuvenation, Steady Growth, Stability, Marked Decline and Catastrophic Decline.

The growth of tourism in Cornwall can certainly be characterised by Butler's model (Figure 1), although the details of development inevitably show deviations.[6]

The Early Development of Coastal Tourism in Cornwall

Walvin has proposed that two major influences – contemporary medical opinion and royal example – affected the early development of coastal tourism within the United Kingdom.[7] Eighteenth-century medical opinion saw sea-water as a cure for many ills, while it became fashionable to emulate George III's enjoyment of sea-bathing.

The earliest response in Cornwall to this demand for access to the sea was in Penzance, which quickly offered itself as a health resort, the first visitor apparently arriving in 1720.[8] However, Bennett has argued that Penzance only developed as a resort of more than local significance in the early nineteenth century. The Napoleonic War restricted access to Mediterranean health resorts, forcing wealthy British invalids to look for alternatives.[9] Penzance's development was based firmly upon publicity concerning its mild climate. The first guidebook to the Penzance district was published in 1815 by a distinguished physician, Dr John Ayrton Paris, who later went on to become President of the Royal College of Physicians. The work contained information for invalids on the climate of Cornwall compared to those of Mediterranean resorts.[10] While Penzance was undoubtedly the pioneering health resort in Cornwall, by 1824 Bude also showed some development, while by 1841 Newquay had acquired some local significance. Other Cornish towns, which were eventually to have an important tourism interest, including St Ives, Fowey, Polperro, Looe, Mevagissey and Boscastle, remained locations dominated by fishing and shipping interests.[11] Visitor numbers continued to increase, with the dominance of Penzance reflected in its physical growth.[12]

Like many other British coastal areas the classic feature of early Cornish seaside tourism was its social exclusivity. Tourism was largely the concern of the affluent, since only they had sufficient leisure time available and could absorb the expense involved. This is not to say that the poorer members of society did not take part in some form of tourism, but any holiday would have been informally organised, a short distance from home and involved little expenditure.[13] Any tourist arriving from outside of Cornwall would almost certainly have belonged to the upper classes, since for all but the most well-off Cornwall's geographical position and limited transport links meant that it was too remote to be a viable destination.

The Coming of the Railway

Walvin has referred to the railway as both 'the fruit and the cause of industrial change',[14] while Walton has attributed its impact on tourism to three important effects. The first of these was the reduction the railway made in journey time and cost, combined with its ability to make new potential destination areas available. Secondly, the railway assisted in the percolation of the seaside tourism habit into the middle class, while, thirdly, it made feasible some working class holidays.[15] As a result the number of seaside visitors in England, generally speaking, began to increase. However, Walton qualifies this by stating that where development was beyond the pull of London middle-class demand, visitor numbers grew less spectacularly.[16] This is certainly true in the case of Cornwall, especially since it was the last county to be connected to the national railway network. Despite this connection in 1859, time and distance still left Cornwall perceived as being remote.[17] This did not prevent Thomas Cook, ever ready for a new opportunity, from conducting his first excursion to Cornwall in 1859.[18]

Walvin, in his major study of early tourism development in Britain, mentions Cornwall only once, stating briefly that:

> Some resorts ... whose railway links came late, or which were too distant for effective day trips, were able to maintain their social aloofness and preserve themselves for a better sort. From Bournemouth into Devon and Cornwall this tended to be the pattern, and poorer visitors did not,

in general, break through into that preserve of the wealthier class, sick and old until the inter-war years.[19]

While Cornwall appeared to lag behind other United Kingdom tourist destination areas in the development of mass tourism up until 1904, this period is still interesting, as some critical debates were taking place within the county.

Sir Arthur Quiller-Couch, an eminent Cornishman of the time, encouraged a debate in 1898 over whether Cornwall should present itself as a tourist destination. The debate took the form of a collection of letters, together with an editorial by Quiller-Couch, in the *Cornish Magazine*.[20] Of the eight published letters five could be described as being moderately to strongly in favour of developing tourism, while three were heavily against the industry. Quiller-Couch's editorial summarises the debate and encapsulates the trauma that many Cornish people were experiencing at the time. First, he identified the social and economic problems that Cornwall faced:

> On the one hand I see Cornwall impoverished by the evil days on which mining ... has fallen. I see her population diminishing and her able bodied sons forced to emigrate by the thousand ... In the presence of destitution and actual famine ... one is bound, if he cares for his countrymen, to consider any cure thoughtfully suggested.

He continued by questioning the social and economic value of the tourist industry:

> And I do see ... that a people which lays itself out to exploit the ... tourist runs an appreciable risk of deterioration in manliness and independence. It may seem a brutal thing to say, but as I had rather be poor myself than subservient, so I would liefer see my countrymen poor than subservient ... Were it within human capacity to decide between a revival of our ancient industries, fishery and mining, and the development of this new business, our decision would be prompt enough. But it is not.
> Well then, since we must cater for the stranger, let us to it well and honestly. Let us respect him and our native land as well.[21]

The debate Quiller-Couch instigated is intriguing, because it might offer evidence for the operation of stages two and three of the Butler model (the point at which the local population considers providing facilities for visitors). At the same time the debate illustrates the increased economic potential that tourism was perceived as offering. Crucially, the debate also throws into sharp relief the influence of Cornish pride on the development of the tourist industry. Tourism was not seen as a favourable alternative to Cornwall's traditional industries, and the development of mass tourism (not yet experienced in Cornwall) was viewed with some disgust. The view that employment in the tourist industry was not 'real work' was already established. This perception can be seen repeatedly throughout the history of the tourist industry in Cornwall.

Yet such discussions and perceptions would almost certainly have remained purely academic were it not for a factor controlled almost entirely from outside Cornwall. For as Mr R. Boase, one of those involved in the Quiller-Couch debate, declared, if tourism was to develop the 'first requisite is accessibility', and that Cornwall 'ought to receive special favour from the Great Western Railway Company'.[22] This proved a remarkable piece of prediction, since six years later Cornwall received both.

1904 Onwards – The Cornish Riviera

The full blast of change associated with the railway was felt with the inauguration of the Cornish Riviera Express in 1904, the culmination of a series of improvements that cut the journey from Paddington Station, London to Penzance to a remarkable seven hours. For the first time Cornwall was remote to English middle-class demand, but 'accessible in its remoteness'.[23]

While a few resorts were arguably called into being by railways, they were almost invariably incidental by-products of schemes designed for other commercial purposes.[24] The mass transportation of tourists was rarely the original purpose. This is true to some extent in Cornwall, with tourism originally something of a by-product. However, the potential value of tourism encouraged the Great Western Railway (the GWR) to take a more pro-active role in the development of Cornish tourism. Eventually it played a considerable part in shaping an image of Cornwall that survives to some extent even today.[25] In addition, the GWR created an important part of the infrastructure of the tourism industry, by opening some of the leading hotels, such as the Tregenna Castle Hotel in St Ives. Similarly, the London and South-West Railway, which was in competition with the GWR, opened the South-Western Hotel in Padstow, to take advantage of its Waterloo to Padstow line.[26] Where the GWR scored heavily over its competitor, however, was in the organisation and effectiveness of its publicity drives to promote Cornwall as a tourist destination area. This was in part due to good co-ordination with certain local towns, such as St Ives and Penzance. However, its major success was in its development of the concept of the 'Cornish Riviera' and the 'Cornish Riviera Express', described by Simmons as a brilliant stroke of publicity.[27] The idea of the 'Cornish Riviera' was based on literary images of place, Celtic legend, and high quality photographs, communicated through poster advertising, newspaper articles and guidebooks. The aim was to produce, in the public's perception, a sub-regional image of Cornwall as being different, and not a part of England.[28] The Cornish, always conscious of their Celtic, rather than Anglo-Saxon, heritage, knew this already, of course! The idea of Cornwall as a land of difference was promulgated through guidebooks produced by the GWR, which were of the highest quality. These were written by well-known authors, such as S.P.B. Mais with his *The Cornish Riviera*.

It is interesting to note that recent tourism researchers, such as Jafari, have identified that tourists seek a holiday in an area that varies considerably from that in which they spend their everyday life.[29] Given that the GWR apparently used this as a marketing tool in the early years of the twentieth century is worth emphasising. The Company's advertising posters were particularly imaginative, and continued either to emphasise Cornwall's difference from England or its similarity to foreign countries. One implored potential tourists to 'See your own country first', and claimed that there were 'Great similarities between Cornwall and Italy in shape, climate and natural beauties.' The evidence for this statement was provided by two maps (one showing Cornwall, the other Italy), with the comparison being aided by the slight distortion of the Lizard peninsula to form a more correct mirror image between Cornwall and Italy. A second poster proclaimed 'Another striking similarity', this time between Cornwall and Brittany – with the evidence being provided in the form of the two St Michael's Mounts. A different poster, and possibly the worst in terms of imagination and quality, showed young women 'Bathing in February in the Cornish Riviera'![30] (Plate 1).

Later posters became more sophisticated, and often appeared more like works of art than advertisements (Plate 2). Potential visitors were encouraged to travel to Cornwall for 'Scenery – Sunshine – Health' on one example, while the Cornish Riviera was projected as 'The Land of Legend and Romance' in another. The GWR also produced posters with the co-operation of specific destinations within Cornwall, such as Penzance, St Ives, Newquay and Looe. However,

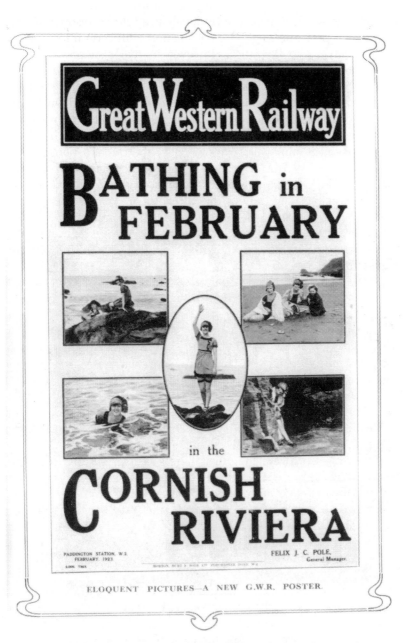

Plate 1. This early poster, with its lack of imagination and clumsy style, demonstrates how the GWR improved with time.

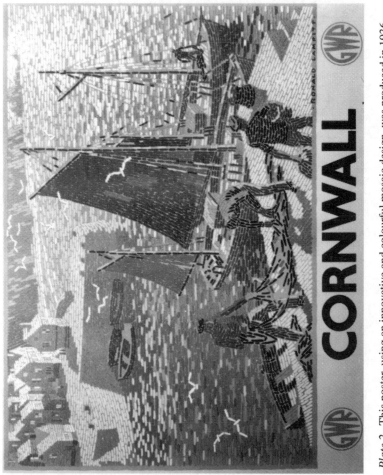

Plate 2. This poster, using an innovative and colourful mosaic design, was produced in 1936. About 1,200 copies were made. The mosaic style, sadly, did not catch on.

the idea of Cornwall as a foreign country remained the unifying theme throughout, as each poster strove through use of light and colour to make Cornwall appear similar to the Mediterranean resorts. All the posters attempted to exude the warmth associated with the romantic class of the French Riviera.[31]

This proved a little too much for Sir Arthur Quiller-Couch, who retorted that Cornwall was not an improvised playground, not a 'Riviera', and the use of that term, whoever first applied it to Cornwall, was a commercial 'inexactitude'. Quiller-Couch's attitude was, however, somewhat confused, since he was quite happy to coin the phrase 'Delectable Duchy'. Others agreed with Quiller-Couch's anti-Riviera stance, stating that 'the essential attributes of Cornwall are in truth the reverse of tropical luxuriance'.[32] However, despite these concerns the potency of the GWR's very imaginative and sophisticated marketing appears to have been considerable. Evidence shows an increase in the Company's passenger receipts between Paddington and the combined Cornish stations of 71 per cent between 1903 and 1913.[33]

The same 1904 watershed in marketing between promoting Cornwall as a health resort and promoting it as a seaside holiday resort can be seen in the guides produced by Penzance. The 1890 *Guide to Penzance* noted its advantages as being:

> Climatically extremely mild, and suitable for invalids; the situation of the town is extremely mild, and sanitary conditions perfect, having an abundant supply of water from two large reservoirs and large filtering beds about two miles from the town...[34]

Another section described no less than 222 interesting antiquities to be seen in the Penzance district.

The 1908 *Guide to Penzance* showed two important variations to the 1890 *Guide*. First, the railway itself is mentioned. Secondly, swimming is described as a 'noble art', to be enjoyed for its own sake, and not as a necessary chore to be completed for reasons of health. The importance of the beach as part of a holiday had begun to be established. By 1926 the nature of Penzance tourism was changing further. Penzance was no longer seen as a destination in itself, but as a gateway to the rest of Cornwall. The idea of visiting one town and remaining there for reasons of health had been replaced by fun on the beach and the chance to explore an area. By 1936 the guide writers had come to recognise the importance of motor cars, and included both Automobile Association and Royal Automobile Club maps, accelerating the process by which touring came to dominate holidays. At the same time the Penzance hotels began to describe themselves in their advertising as offering: 'The Maximum of Comforts, [the] Minimum of Cost'. At the same time advertisements for smaller accommodation units (such as bed and breakfast) appeared, suggesting that Cornwall was beginning to experience the arrival of a more cost-conscious clientele.

No longer the sole domain of the affluent, middle and even some working class tourists were seeking holidays in Cornwall. The nature of tourism had by now completed its transformation. The beach, rather than antiquities, formed the basis of most holidays' activity contents. The 1936 Penzance *Guide* went so far as to proclaim that: 'Clad only in the minimum necessary for decency, one can sprawl in the sun after one's bathe with the utmost benefit.'[35]

The Economic and Social Impact of Seaside Tourism in the Twentieth Century

The impact of élitist health tourism in Cornwall had been limited to specific areas. Penzance, as the main provider, experienced the greatest changes, growing in size and population. The development of mass beach-based tourism produced new effects. First, there were increasing numbers of tourists arriving in the early decades of the twentieth century. Secondly, their behaviour was changing. Instead of being predominantly sedentary, and spending most of their money in one town, the tourists were touring larger areas of Cornwall. As a result tourist expenditure had an impact on a larger number of towns. This had effects on both the economy of Cornwall and spurred the development of more Cornish towns having a tourism interest.

Shaw and Williams have argued that with an expansion in demand for seaside tourism in the twentieth century the tourist industry in Cornwall became far more commercially aware than it had been in the nineteenth century.[36] This increased demand for tourism was the result of a number of critical developments in the inter-war years. Of particular importance was the increasing number of firms in England and Wales that were prepared to offer their workers paid holiday leave, so that by 1939 11 million workers were entitled to holidays with pay.[37] However, the Second World War inevitably delayed some of these changes.

The increasing numbers of tourists encouraged many towns in Cornwall to swiftly transform their economies towards service activities, as seen in Table 1. This process was aided by a general

trend towards de-industrialisation, described in depth by Payton, as
the tin mining and engineering industries began to fail.[38]

Table 1
Employment in Personal Service in Cornwall, 1911-1951

Administrative Area	Total Occupied Population of each Area (per cent)			
	1911	1921	1931	1951
Bude-Stratton U.D	-	32.1	-	20.0
Falmouth M.B	17.2	17.1	21.0	13.3
Fowey M.B	-	-	20.6	16.7
Newquay U.D	-	29.4	24.1	27.8
Padstow U.D	-	16.2	12.8	14.1
Penzance U.D	18.2	22.6	22.6	13.4
St Austell U.D	-	32.1	-	10.9
St Ives M.B	13.9	16.2	21.4	20.7
Truro M.B	16.5	17.5	18.1	12.9
Cornwall	13.8	13.9	15.2	10.8
England and Wales	12.8	11.7	12.7	9.4

Notes:
1. The figures relate to the administrative areas as constituted at the
time of the various censuses.
2. The definition of personal service has been subject to change over
time. For 1911 it included domestic servants, servants in hotels and
eating houses, gamekeepers, caretakers, servants in institutions,
laundry workers among others. For 1921 and 1931 it also included
lodging house and boarding house keepers, restaurant keepers, hotel
keepers, publicans and beer sellers. For 1951 dry cleaners, barbers and
matrons of institutions were added to the above definitions.

Source: H. Heck, *Survey of the Holiday Industry* (Truro, Cornwall
County Council, 1966).

Of special note in Table 1 is the importance service industry
occupations had in specific local areas, namely the tourist destination
areas. For example, by 1951 service employment accounted for 27.8
and 20.7 per cent of all jobs in Newquay and St Ives, respectively,
compared to the average service employment of 9.4 per cent for
England and Wales as a whole.

The development of the Cornish tourist industry from the early twentieth century also had significant consequences for the spatial distribution of population in the county. The growth of employment in tourist destination areas, coupled with the developing popularity of the seaside for retirement locations, led to a definite shift in population towards coastal parishes, as shown by Table 2:

Table 2
Population Distribution in the Cornish Coastal Parishes, 1901-1961

Years of Census	Population[a]		Population Change (per cent)	
	Cornwall	Coastal Parishes	Cornwall	Coastal Parishes
1901	320,000	127,000	-	-
1911	326,000	128,000	+1.8	+0.8
1921	313,000[b]	124,800[b]	-3.9	-2.5
1931	335,400	(128,800 178,000[c])	+0.7	+3.2
1951	338,200	196,000	+6.3	+10.0[c]
1961	338,200	198,400	+0.9	+1.2
Total Change 1901-1961			+5.6	+12.5[c]

[a] Population as enumerated in the censuses, excluding defence establishments.
[b] Because the 1921 census was taken in June an abnormally large number of holiday visitors, estimated at 5,100, were enumerated; these have been excluded from the tabulated figures.
[c] The effect of the boundary changes of 1934 has been excluded from the later figures of population change.

Source: H. Heck, *Survey of the Holiday Industry* (Truro, Cornwall County Council, 1966).

As Cornish tourism developed into a powerful force for economic and social change, it can be of little surprise that it began to exert an influence on the morphology of those areas where it was focused.

Developments in the Tourist Destination Areas

The morphology of the Cornish towns and areas affected by tourism in the twentieth century are quite unusual when compared to other resort areas in England and Wales. Bennett has attempted to create a threefold classification of destination areas in the county.[39] This classification, with some modifications, was to form the basis for the categorisation of destination areas in the important survey later conducted by the County Council.[40] As a result it has generally become recognised as the accepted classification for Cornwall.

The first part of the classification concerned 'new holiday towns', defined as towns where an original small coastal settlement, in an environment of insufficient planning control, had developed to such an extent that the original nuclei had been reduced to insignificance. Such a destination can be seen as reflecting the traditional working-class seaside holiday resort, as visualised by Urry.[41] These sites are geared to catering for beach-based mass tourism. Although they are often referred to as traditional resorts they are in fact, architecturally, relatively recent constructions. Within Cornwall only Newquay, and possibly Bude, can be realistically seen as conforming to this model.

The second element considered were the old ports, fishing centres or towns with an 'important tourist interest'. In other words, existing settlements where mass tourism had not extinguished the original nature of the settlement. Penzance, Padstow, St Ives and Falmouth, for example, all fall within this category. Padstow has been more fully analysed by Gilligan.[42] He noted that in this north Cornwall town the tourist industry at first developed slowly, due to Padstow's late connection to the railway. But eventually tourism became a significant element in the local economy, seemingly used to bolster economic income as the shipping industry stuttered. In some ways Padstow and similar towns' experiences of tourism are those of Cornwall as a whole, albeit in microcosm.

Since this type of town constitutes an important part of the seaside tourist industry in Cornwall, it is worth speculating on the reasons for its development. Factors from both the demand and supply side of the tourism industry might be identified as possible explanations. On the demand side Cornwall was for a long time too remote from the large London and Midlands population centres to attract tourists looking for shorter holidays. Other resorts in closer proximity and with superior railway links (at least initially) were able to better serve this market of middle and working class excursionists.[43] Cornwall, on the other hand, continued to cater to a smaller number of tourists who would have probably stayed for a longer period of time (perhaps for reasons of health). Even with the 'Cornish Riviera Express' Cornwall's relative remoteness to the centres of population resulted in more expensive rail tickets, which dictated it should remain exclusive to some degree.

On the supply side the policies and attitudes of many in the seaside towns towards the tourist industry reflected the wider Cornish attitude to tourism. If Cornish pride initially worked against tourism until Cornwall was forced into it by economic circumstances, the same pride later determined that Cornwall had to be a destination area with a difference. Such attitudes are recognisable, for example, in the guides produced for Penzance and its district. The 1960 *Guide* informed the reader that, 'When you come to Penzance, you do much more than come to a seaside resort with a beach, a pier and the usual trappings'.[44] While in 1973 Penzance was described as having: 'an individuality that never fails to appeal'.[45] The 1981 *Guide* considered the town to be 'the resort with character'.[46]

The final element in the classification of tourist destinations were the 'new centres of the holiday industry'. Included in this were chalets, caravans and camping sites. It appears they might have been the cause of some of the more recent antagonism towards tourism within the county. These new accommodation developments were identified by Shaw and Williams as the response of the now more commercially aware Cornish holiday industry towards attracting the growing market for mass tourism seaside holidays (offered at a lower price).[47] The key feature of this new market was their use of motor cars and not the train. With the arrival of the car-borne tourist the influence of the GWR quickly waned. The marketing of Cornwall lost its unifying factor, with different, even contrasting, images being projected. The broader market brought with it a demand for cheaper accommodation, met in a good part by chalets, caravans and camp-sites. In Cornwall the number of chalets and static caravans increased by 310 and 240 per cent respectively between 1954 and 1964.[48] This trend is also reflected in the increase in visitor numbers arriving in Cornwall between 1954 and 1978, as illustrated in Figure 2.

Figure 2
Numbers of Visitors to Cornwall, 1954-1987

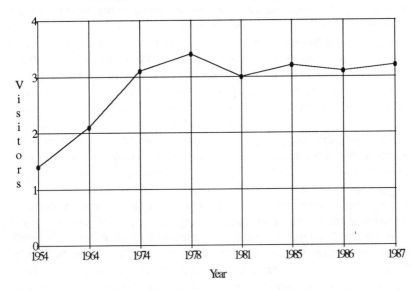

Source: Data from Cornwall County Council Planning Department.

It may be that the increasing number of visitors, and the construction of the larger facilities needed to accommodate them, in the post-Second World War period, marks the point of origin of the increasingly acrimonious conflicts that arose between the county's tourism industry and some members of the local community. In these post-war decades many local people came to question, socially, economically and environmentally, the role and value of the county's tourist industry.[49]

Tourism Faces Increasing Controls

The post-Second World War period in Cornwall thus witnessed a growth in visitor numbers, with a peak in the 1970s, coupled with an increasing antagonism between the tourist industry and the local community. Both suggest the entering of the 'Consolidation' and eventually the 'Stagnation' phases of the resort cycle model. It is to this increasing hostility between the Cornish tourist industry and some sections of the local community that attention will now be turned.

Concern over the social and environmental impacts of tourism was reflected in the greater attention official planners paid to the tourist industry. The 1950s and 1960s was a period when visitor numbers appeared to be rising inexorably. Naturally, in this situation, the local government planners' attention was on control. The attitude of planners towards tourism began subtly to change. This change was reflected initially in attempts to prevent tourism from creating excessive environmental damage. Later, planners became more critical of tourism's social and economic influence on Cornwall.

The 1966 Heck Report, conducted by the county planning department, summed up succinctly the new preoccupation with preventing environmental damage: 'Unless carefully guided the holiday industry itself could contribute to the destruction of the very features that attract visitors.'[50] This also illustrates a realistic view of what damage the tourist industry was capable of.

Soon after the 1950s planners began to declare tourist 'saturation areas'. These were areas where planners felt any further increase in the concentration and number of tourists was environmentally inadvisable. The first, in 1959, surrounded Looe on Cornwall's south coast, while the 1960s saw most of the north coast from St Ives to Newquay covered in this fashion. The battle between the tourist industry and planners had been joined in earnest, such that by 1962 85 per cent of the total coastline of Cornwall was subject to some kind of planning control.[51]

As well as the damage that tourism was allegedly exerting on the county's environment, concerns arose over the possibility of it being a prime catalyst in the destruction of Cornwall's social fabric. Of particular concern was the role it was felt to have in encouraging the development of 'second homes' and 'seasonally occupied properties'. These are properties used by people from outside Cornwall as holiday homes, which meant that local people had to compete with outsiders for a limited number of houses. That Cornwall was in a relatively weak economic situation meant that the locals were relatively less financially equipped to compete with the outsiders for properties whose value had been artificially inflated. Tourism was blamed for encouraging a large throughput of relatively wealthier visitors who, having enjoyed a holiday in Cornwall, then wished to purchase their own permanent base. Local people, unable to find somewhere to live, either had to leave the county or share with relatives (living with parents, for example) creating a 'hidden homelessness'.[52] Interestingly many of these problems had been identified as far back as 1936, by none other than Sir Arthur Quiller-Couch, the former tourism proponent, who argued:

Worst of all is the man who, coming to a beauty-spot with some money in his pocket, tells himself – 'what a charming place for a little pied-à-terre which I can use in July-August ...' The process began with his securing a cottage by outbidding a young couple of 'natives' eager to marry and set up house in the one cottage to let within their reach. Nowadays he can buy a cheap, pink-tiled bungalow from a mass-producing firm, bargain for the spot which pleases him most [and] deface it for thousands... I admit, of course, that the need of an impoverished countryside will abet him in this; but there remains a distinction between those who commit or aid in offences and those through whom the offences come.[53]

The final criticism of the tourist industry was economic, in particular over the nature of the employment it created. The industry found itself criticised in structure plans and faced with cost/benefit analyses, such as that conducted by Lewes for the then Southwest Economic Planning Council in 1970.[54] For example, the County Council associated tourism employment with 'very wide seasonal fluctuations, ... vulnerability to economic recession and relatively low rates of pay'.[55] The lack of a definable career structure re-energised the old complaint that work in the tourist industry was not 'real work'. Worries were also voiced over the proportion of in-migrants who were employed in the industry, instead of locals.[56] There is some more recent evidence that suggests that ownership of tourist-related businesses is dominated by people who come from outside of Cornwall. Williams, Shaw and Greenwood, for instance, found in a large study of the ownership and operating characteristics of tourist businesses in Cornwall, that only one-third of tourism entrepreneurs were born in Cornwall.[57] In fact, the origin of entrepreneurs by region closely resembled the origin of tourists to Cornwall, suggesting that there might be a process of 'tourist to tourism entrepreneur'.[58] Furthermore, many owners of tourist accommodation were as interested in being 'consumers' of tourism as being 'producers', with many expressing social reasons, such as a desire to 'get out of the rat-race', as being more important business motivations than 'profit maximisation'.[59]

Other costs were also identified – an early County Structure Plan Document noted that 'the seasonal nature of tourism gives rise to abnormally high costs in providing facilities in relation to the short period for which they are used'.[60] This claim weakened the view that tourism was a sound generator of profit.

The Cornish tourism industry itself, faced with problems and costs that appeared glaringly obvious, and suffering from near statistical invisibility in terms of its benefits, fought back with studies of its own. The main argument *of The Economic and Social Impact of Tourism in Cornwall*, published in 1976, for example, was that costs and benefits needed to be placed in their true perspective before any evaluation could be made. It also attempted to challenge what it described as the strong and widespread misconceptions prevalent about the industry.[61] Later studies have given some indication of the importance of the tourist industry's multiplier effects on the county's economy. A study of Looe, for example, found that 83 per cent of businesses contacted considered tourism to be either 'beneficial' or 'very beneficial'. Moreover, the extent of perceived benefit was far greater than merely the accommodation or specialist retail sectors, with even 27 per cent of manufacturing firms viewing it as 'very beneficial'.[62]

The importance of these multipliers magnified concerns when in the late 1970s visitor numbers began to stagnate, levelling off at about the three million mark (see Figure 2).[63] Under the pressure of foreign competition support for the tourism industry rallied, with one local government officer describing the resources invested in tourism promotion as being 'peanuts'.[64] However, despite this the Cornish tourism industry is still subject to heavy criticism, notably in the recent work by Deacon, George and Perry, *Cornwall at the Cross-roads?*.[65]

Most worrying of all to the industry is the belief held by some writers that to recover from the trough tourism has recently found itself in will require more than a re-investment in a simple facelift or increased marketing. Perry has argued that the industry's problems stem from the demise of the conventional family summer holiday by the British seaside, a national trend that has been gathering momentum since the early 1970s. He has argued that, 'It [family beach holidays in Britain] has had a good run for its money but, like all mass consumer products, its commercial life was limited and for more than a decade the writing has been on the wall'.[66]

Any Future for Cornish Tourism?

Urry in his book, *The Tourist Gaze*, has stressed the fundamentally visual nature of the tourism experience. If tourism provides a 'social therapy ... [a] valve that maintains the world in good running order', by allowing a brief escape from everyday life, then, Urry argues, the main characteristic of the tourist's destination area is a visual contrast to his or her home-world.[67] Urry also argues that it is the unusualness of the visual environment that places other tourist activities and experiences in a different context from ordinary life.[68]

On this basis, Urry has questioned why so many tourists have now come to see the spending of a week or fortnight in a traditional United Kingdom resort as an unattractive tourist experience. He claims the answer lies in a socio-economic transformation of British society. Accordingly, 'very broadly speaking "mass holiday-making" to the British seaside resort was the quintessential form of tourism in an industrial society'.[69] By its nature mass tourism was an activity that presupposed regulated and organised work. Thus with the development of a post-industrial society it is no surprise that new forms of tourism should develop in response. Urry has labelled the new holiday-making as 'post-tourism'.

For the traditional seaside resorts the greatest marketing problem to overcome is that they are no longer extra-ordinary, compared to the tourist's everyday, ordinary life. The tourist's ordinary world in the United Kingdom is no longer dominated by smoke-stack industries, while changes in the spatial distribution of entertainment has meant that services previously available only in the traditional tourist destination areas, are now available universally (accelerated by the availability of television). At the same time, traditional resorts, which are actually of a relatively new construction, lack an historic manufacturing base, paradoxically now seen by the tourist as unusual, and in contrast to their home areas. The traditional resorts tend to lack interesting sites to be packaged, sacralized and gazed upon. There is some evidence for Urry's arguments. Eastbourne, for example, has pursued what Lean has described as an inland road to revival by portraying itself as an architecturally historic town and reducing the role played by the sea in its marketing.[70] However, many traditional United Kingdom resorts do not have this option available.

While Urry's arguments are quite convincing, it would be unwise to ignore the effect of the development of foreign competition, in particular those new destination areas that offer guaranteed sun. However, it is also important not to overstress the decline of domestic British tourism. During 1993 British residents spent £8,425 million on domestic holiday tourism and made 91 million tourist trips within the United Kingdom.[71] At the same time traditional destination areas are losing some of their importance. This suggests that United Kingdom tourism is not simply declining, but going through a more complicated trend involving a period of restructuring.[72]

One explanation may lie in the increasing number of holidays that tourists are taking, and the development of 'travel portfolios', where:

> A weekend walking the hills or experiencing an historic city often rounded out a portfolio for a privileged elite, which might also include 10 days of skiing and two weeks in Thailand. Lower down the social scale it might be day excursions to nearby attractions that rounded out a portfolio centred on two weeks of sunshine in Florida or the Mediterranean region.[73]

In summary, domestic British tourism has in recent years gone through some major changes in terms of the 'demand' side of the industry. As a result the 'supply' side of the industry is also changing. The idea of a travel portfolio suggests that modern tourists may seek to take more than one holiday in a year: a main holiday and one or more additional holidays. The suggestion is that the creation of new destination areas in the United Kingdom – such as the historic city offering cultural or heritage tourism – is a response to the demand for additional holidays. Main beach-based holidays, for which the traditional United Kingdom resorts are designed to attract, are increasingly being taken abroad in countries that can guarantee sunshine and, in some cases, lower prices. Traditional destination areas are faced with the problem of either converting to cater for the new forms of tourism, for which they are generally poorly equipped, or convincing an uncertain clientele that they are worthy of visiting. Thus they are faced with either rejuvenation or decline.

There is evidence for this desire to seek different holiday experiences in the United Kingdom. Middleton and O'Brien, for example, have found that the British short-break market in the late 1980s was growing at 20 per cent per annum, with a discernible skewing of the clientele towards the A, B and C1 socio-economic groups.[74] A greater willingness, or ability, amongst these social groups to spend money on tourism has also been identified by Seaton.[75]

As an area used to marketing itself as a mass-tourism destination the expectation would be that Cornwall now faces a decline in visitor numbers. Both the resort cycle and Urry's theories suggest that this trend is almost inevitable. But before drawing conclusions it is important to bear in mind that applying any theory to Cornwall is problematic. For example, Cornwall has the beaches required for seaside tourism, and these have come to dominate its marketing strategy. However, it also has an abundance of interesting heritage features and a relict manufacturing landscape that could be used to take advantage of the new heritage tourism market. Those researchers predicting the decline of mass tourist resorts assume that because they are of a relatively recent construction they will be unable to offer a heritage tourism product. Cornwall is extremely lucky: because mass tourism arrived late, developed slowly and was never fully embraced as the basis of many towns' economies, those towns have retained their character. Some towns have already adopted, at least in part, the heritage tourism industry. St Ives, for example, now contains the very successful 'Tate of the West' art gallery, which has re-established the success of their holiday industry. This has led some commentators to call on Cornwall to 'stop trying to dig for victory with the bucket and spade brigade and seek to meet ... competition with a move upmarket'.[76]

The idea of tourism marketing moving towards heritage tourism is attractive. Lowenthal has argued that, 'if the past is a foreign country, nostalgia has made it the foreign country with the healthiest tourist trade of all'.[77] The irony is that the heritage tourism market is associated with more affluent tourists. Cornwall may well return to trying to attract the same type of discerning tourist that the Great Western Railway sought in the early years of the twentieth century.

NOTES

1   G. Shaw, A. Williams and A. Griffiths, *The Cornwall Holiday Survey, 1993* (University of Exeter, Tourism Research Group, 1994).

2   Cornwall Country Council, *Cornwall Structure Plan Explanatory Memorandum: Incorporating the First Alteration* (Truro, Cornwall County Council, 1994), 10.

3   R. Butler, 'The concept of a tourism area cycle of evolution: implications for management of tourism resources', *Canadian Geographer*, 24, 1 (1982), 5-12.

4   *Ibid.*

5   *Ibid.*

6   G. Shaw and A. Williams, 'From bathing hut to theme-park: tourism development in Southwest England', *Journal of Regional Studies*, 11, 1-2 (1991), 16-31.

7   J.K. Walvin, *Beside the Seaside* (London, 1978), chap.1.

8   W. Bennett, 'The origins and development of the tourism industry in Cornwall', *Royal Cornwall Polytechnic Society Annual Report* (1949), 32-53.

9   *Ibid.*, 34.
10 R. Pearse, *The Land Beside the Celtic Sea: Aspects of Cornwall's Past* (Cornwall, Truran, 1983), 99.
11 Bennett, *Tourism Industry in Cornwall*, 36-7.
12 *Ibid.*, 35.
13 J. Towner, 'What is tourism's history?', *Tourism Management*, 16, 5 (1995) 339-43.
14 Walvin, *Beside the Seaside*, chap.2.
15 J. Walton, *The English Seaside Resort: a Social History, 1750-1914* (Leicester, 1978), 22.
16 *Ibid.*, chap.3.
17 J. Simmons, 'The railway in Cornwall, 1835-1914', *Journal of the Royal Institution of Cornwall* (1982), 11-29.
18 *Ibid.*, 18.
19 Walvin, *Beside the Seaside*, 88-9.
20 A. Quiller-Couch, 'How to develop Cornwall as a tourist resort', *Cornish Magazine* (1898), 237.
21 *Ibid.*
22 R. Boase, 'How to develop Cornwall as a tourist resort', *Cornish Magazine* (1898), 158.
23 K. Robbins, *Nineteenth-Century England and Wales: The Making of a Nation* (Oxford, Oxford University Press, 1989), 25.
24 Walvin, *Beside the Seaside*, chap.3.
25 P. Payton and P. Thornton, 'The Great Western Railway and the Cornish-Celtic revival', *Cornish Studies*, 3 (1995), 83-103.
26 Simmons, *Railway in Cornwall*, 25.
27 *Ibid.*, 22.
28 B. Brown, 'Developments in the promotion of major seaside resorts: how to effect a transition by really making an effort', in B. Goodall and G. Ashworth, eds, *Marketing in the Tourism Industry: the Promotion of Major Destination Regions* (London, Routledge, 1988), 176-84.
29 J. Jafari, 'Socio-cultural dimensions of tourism: an English literature review', in J. Bustrzanowski, ed., *Tourism as a Factor of Change* (Vienna, Economic Co-ordination Centre for Research and Documentation in Social Sciences, 1989), 17-60.
30 R. Wilson, *Go Great Western* (Newton Abbot, David and Charles, 1970, republished 1987).
31 B. Cole and R. Durack, *Railway Posters, 1923-1947* (London, Lawrence King, 1992), chap.2.
32 A.K. Hamilton Jenkin, *Cornwall and its People* (Newton Abbot, David and Charles, 1983, republished from 1932-3), Introduction, v.

33 Simmons, *Railway in Cornwall*, 26.

34 *Guide to Penzance* (1890).

35 *Guide to Penzance* (1908, 1926, 1936).

36 Shaw and Williams, 'Bathing hut to theme park', 18.

37 Walvin, *Beside the Seaside*, 110.

38 P. Payton, *The Making of Modern Cornwall* (Redruth, Truran, 1992), chap.5.

39 Bennett, *Tourism Industry in Cornwall*, 44.

40 H. Heck, *Survey of the Holiday Industry* (Truro, Cornwall County Council, 1966).

41 J. Urry, *The Tourist Gaze: Leisure and Travel in Contemporary Societies* (London, Sage, 1990).

42 H. Gilligan, 'Visitors, tourists and outsiders in a Cornish town', in M. Bouquet and M. Winter, eds, *Who From Their Labours Rest?* (Aldershot, Avebury, 1987), 65-83.

43 Shaw and Williams, 'Bathing hut to theme-park', 17.

44 *Guide to Penzance*, 1960.

45 *Guide to Penzance*, 1973.

46 *Guide to Penzance*, 1981.

47 Shaw and Williams, 'Bathing hut to theme-park', 22.

48 *Ibid.*

49 *Ibid.*

50 Heck, *Survey of the Holiday Industry*, 1.

51 Shaw and Williams, 'Bathing hut to theme-park', 22.

52 M. Williams, 'Housing the Cornish', in P. Payton, ed., *Cornwall Since the War* (Redruth, Institute of Cornish Studies, Truran, 1993), 157-81.

53 A. Quiller-Couch, 'What has been done - what can be done', *Council for the Protection of Rural England*, Cornish Branch (1936).

54 F. Lewes, A. Culyer and G. Brady, *The Holiday Industry of Devon and Cornwall: A Report Prepared for the Southwest Economic Planning Council* (London, HMSO, 1970); see also, Cornwall County Council, *Cornwall Structure Plan Project Report* (Truro, Cornwall County Council, 1975).

55 Cornwall County Council, *Structure Plan Policy Choice Consultation Document* (Truro, Cornwall County Council, 1976), 36.

56 Cornwall County Council, *Cornwall Structure Plan Project Report* (Truro, Cornwall County Council, 1975), 99.

57 A. Williams, G. Shaw and J. Greenwood, 'From tourist to tourism entrepreneur, from consumption to production: evidence from Cornwall, England', *Environment and Planning A*, 21 (1989), 1639-53.

58   *Ibid.*, 1639.
59   G. Shaw and A. Williams, 'Tourism and employment: reflections on a pilot study of Looe, Cornwall', *Area*, 20, 1 (1988), 21-34.
60   *Cornwall Structure Plan Project Report*, 36.
61   Business and Economic Planning on behalf of the Cornwall Tourism Consultative Committee, *The Economic and Social Impact of Tourism on Cornwall* (St Columb, Cornwall, Edyvean, 1976).
62   G. Shaw, A. Williams and J. Greenwood, 'Comparative studies in local economies: the Cornish case', *Built Environment*, 13, 2 (1987), 73-84.
63   Information kindly supplied by Cornwall County Council Planning Department.
64   Alan Bruce (Economic Development Officer for Kerrier District Council), *Western Morning News*, 8 November 1993.
65   B. Deacon, A. George and R. Perry, *Cornwall at the Crossroads?* (Redruth, Earles Press, 1988).
66   R. Perry, 'Cultural tourism in Cornwall', in A. Williams and G. Shaw, eds, *Tourism Research Group Papers, 4, Tourism and Development: Overviews and Case Studies of the United Kingdom and Southwest Region* (Department of Geography, University of Exeter, 1987).
67   J. Urry, 'The tourist gaze revisited', *American Behavioral Scientist*, 36, 2 (1993), 172-87; see also, J. Krippendorf, *The Holiday Makers: Understanding the Impact of Leisure and Travel* (London, Heinemann, 1989).
68   Urry, *The Tourist Gaze*, chap.1.
69   J. Urry, 'Some social and spatial aspects of services', *Environment and Planning D: Society and Space*, 5, 5-26.
70   G. Lean, 'Seaside resorts take an inland road to revival', *Independent on Sunday*, 5 June 1994, 6.
71   British Tourist Authority/English Tourist Board/Wales Tourist Board/Scottish Tourist Board/Northern Ireland Tourist Board, *United Kingdom Tourist Statistics, 1993* (London, British Tourist Authority, 1994).
72   R. Prentice, *Tourism and Heritage Attractions* (London, Routledge, 1993), 2.
73   A. Williams and G. Shaw, 'Tourism research', *American Behavioral Scientist*, 36, 2 (1992), 135.
74   V. Middleton and K. O'Brien, 'Short break holidays in the United Kingdom: packaging and marketing the fastest growing sector of the UK holiday market', *Travel and Tourism Analyst* (May 1987), 45-54.

75   A. Seaton, 'Social stratification in tourism choice and experience since the war', *Tourism Management* (March 1992), 106-11.
76   O. Bowcott, 'Tourism declines as more holiday abroad', *The Guardian*, 28 July 1994, 9.
77   D. Lowenthal, *The Past is a Foreign Country* (Cambridge University Press, 1985).

SEASIDE RESORT STRATEGIES : THE CASE OF INTER-WAR TORQUAY

Nigel Morgan

The period 1918-1939 saw far reaching changes in British society, changes which were reflected in its holiday industry and which created new challenges for many seaside resorts. The period witnessed the consolidation of the British seaside industry and also, of critical importance, the appearance of recognisably modern resort activities, especially in the field of promotion. This was particularly the case in Devon, where the shape assumed by the tourism industry in the inter-war period was to remain substantially unaltered for over fifty years. By examining in some detail the resort promotion strategies employed by Devon's major resort, that of Torquay, it is possible to illustrate this establishment of modern resort activities. Indeed, during the inter-war years, Torquay Borough Council's resort promotion strategies played a vital role in the development of Torquay as one of Europe's most prominent seaside resorts.[1]

Seaside Tourism in Devon, 1918-1939

This was a period of tremendous upheaval in British society. The First World War and its aftermath had radically transformed European society and in the roaring twenties people indulged in modern forms of leisure on an unprecedented scale. In these decades Britain's leisure industry hugely expanded, and whilst other sectors of the economy faltered, Britain's seaside resorts invested heavily in major capital projects, creating parks, laying out expansive promenades and building impressive facilities such as pavilions, theatres, bandstands and winter gardens. Cinemas and amusement arcades sprang up in seaside towns across the country and, whilst there were few grand hotels built, family hotels prospered.[2] Of the considerable inter-war capital investment in Britain's seaside tourism industry, much of it was concentrated in Devon, particularly in Torquay itself. Such investment contributed to the rise of Devon's resorts, a rise reflected in the fact that the greatest population growth in the county at this time was along the coastal belt.[3]

The arrival of the motor car and the charabanc was crucial in changing British holidaymaking patterns in these years. Although the real democratisation of this form of transport had to wait until after the Second World War, it nevertheless had a dramatic impact in the inter-war period. In the early twenties the emergence of motor vehicles as a competitor to the railways meant that holidaymakers could, for the first time, reach destinations previously only accessible by rail (see Plate 1). In Devon, an area remote from large population centres, this meant that in the years after the First World War much of the county was now opened up to working class travellers by the advent of the motor coach tours.[4]

This had major implications for Devon's resorts. First, as increased motor transport began to enable visitors to travel between resorts, the rivalry between them increased and advertising became an important area of activity for competing destinations.[5] Secondly, the inter-war years, particularly the thirties, emerge as key decades of conflict within the resorts themselves. This saw some increase in the overall real income of the British working class and a nascent consumer revolution, itself part of the general long-term move from a production to a consumption culture in Britain. It was, therefore, a decade when Devon experienced considerable pressure from the rising influx of holidaymakers. Devon's natural resources of coastline and moors came under increasing pressure from visitor numbers and its resort communities faced decisions over whether to encourage or to oppose this shift, as one local newspaper put it, from 'the classes to the masses'.[6] The decisions made by these resort communities in the twenties and thirties had a fundamental impact on the future development of the resorts' tourism industries in the twentieth century. The different paths chosen by resorts such as Torquay, Ilfracombe, Sidmouth and Exmouth clearly illustrate the emergence of differing resort strategies in this period.

In 1900 Torquay, with its population of 30,000, was the only major Devon resort, accompanied by just over a half a dozen medium-sized ones and a number of minor ones. At this date Torquay still attracted titled visitors, especially during the winter months. The other Devon resorts were established as watering-places which attracted a broad section of middle-class tourists whilst still resisting large-scale influxes of working class visitors. All of the Devon resorts were 'select' and 'respectable' and whilst social gradations did exist they ranged only from middle-class Ilfracombe to the more genteel Torquay. Even Ilfracombe, drawing trippers from South Wales and Bristol, catered principally for a middle-class market, and Exmouth, attracting more trippers than any other resort

Torquay and some Devon Seaside Resorts

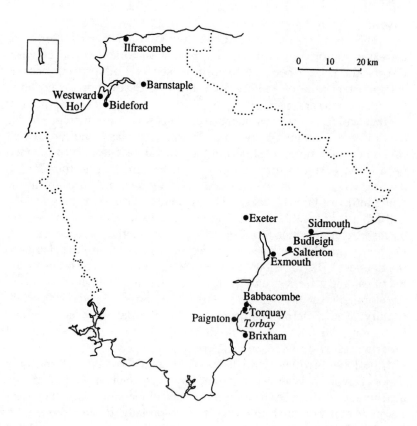

Plate 1. The increasing democratisation of tourism. This charabanc leaving Ilfracombe in 1919 was one of many which enabled holidaymakers to reach destinations previously accessible only by rail. (Ilfracombe Museum)

in south Devon, only drew about 4,000 each year, a tenth of the day-trip trade of Weston-Super-Mare. Working class trippers found it difficult to visit Devon as few had the resources to reach its resorts, all of which also shunned the more popular amusements which would have attracted such a clientele.[7] This meant that the Devon resorts' distance from major centres of working class population ensured that those resorts with a controlling interest favouring a 'select' clientele were able to pursue exclusionist policies until after the Second World War. In fact, although the inter-war years and the ensuing decades witnessed a broadening of their clientele, the most interesting feature of the development of Devon resorts in the second half of the twentieth century is the length of time they retained their relatively 'select' character.

Resort Strategies in Devon

Although it may appear somewhat anachronistic to refer to early twentieth-century local authority resort strategies, the evidence clearly indicates that key players in the resort communities were actively pursuing definite policies to secure certain market positions for their resorts. A range of strategies actually emerged in Devon. For example, Ilfracombe, Paignton and Exmouth pursued similar policies, actively engaging in promotional activities and in the provision of tourism facilities to attract a relatively broad base of tourist. At the other end of the spectrum were resorts such as Sidmouth and Budleigh Salterton in South Devon. Sidmouth, in particular, provides an excellent example of a resort where the controlling groups in the community consciously pursued policies designed to exclude certain types of tourist. Whilst the local council did invest in some new facilities, activity was minimal and it declined to organise any entertainments, the life-blood of resorts such as Torquay and Ilfracombe. Minimal sums were also spent by the local authority on advertising, the resort preferring to rely on the efforts of the town's score or so of luxury hotels.[8]

As we have seen, the distance of Devon's resorts from the major centres of urban population enabled the resorts' controlling groups to manipulate holidaymakers' access to and use of leisure space. Indeed, residential opposition defeated several moves to open up areas of Devon to the lower middle and the working classes in these years. Some of the more striking examples of the attempts to control 'undesirable' tourism developments in Devon at this time include the opposition to Sunday concerts, the running of Sunday steamers and charabancs and the opening of municipal leisure facilities on

Sundays.[9] There was also the successful opposition in 1939 to schemes to develop two holiday camps, one in the north at Westward Ho! and one in the south at Rousdon.[10] Even more typical of this continuing control of leisure behaviour, was the local authority restrictions placed on charabanc tours, mainly patronised by working class tourists.[11] In opposing these developments, the local residents, ratepayers and those with vested interests in existing tourism businesses articulated fears, not only of competition to established businesses, but also of their possible effects on the social tone of the resorts. Moreover, having seen that working class access to the resorts was constrained by the economic barrier of distance, some of the more 'select' Devon resorts, notably Sidmouth and Budleigh Salterton, actively discouraged improvements to the railway network to prevent further influxes of tourists.[12]

Torquay's Resort Strategies, 1918-1939

In the nineteenth century Torquay had developed into a major health and retirement centre, expanding especially rapidly between the 1840s and 1860s. In these years it attracted an aristocratic clientele which built prestigious villas and first created Torquay's reputation for fashionability.[13] By the early twentieth century, however, the town had also begun to attract visitors seeking entertainment as well as those who sought recuperation, and during the years to 1914 this trend led to the town council building several impressive tourist facilities, not least of which was an elegant new pavilion overlooking the seafront, completed in 1913.[14]

Following this period of heavy municipal investment before the War, the inter-war years were to prove even more critical in the shaping of twentieth-century Torquay. These years witnessed the realignment of the resort's image, as its era as a select watering-place drew to a close and its rise as a more 'popular' holiday resort began. Unlike its rivals within Devon, however, Torquay was able to draw its clientele from a much broader economic and geographic range, concentrating on the prosperous regions of the South-East and the Midlands, the populations of which were benefiting from rising real incomes in this period. Torquay's broader appeal was due to a number of factors, particularly its diversity of functions as a town, its excellent communications network and the policies of its local authority, all of which combined to enable Torquay to ride out the inter-war depression years more effectively than its main Devon rival, Ilfracombe. Whereas at the beginning of the century the two resorts had been very similarly matched in terms of the facilities they offered and their accommodation base, by 1939 Torquay had significantly pulled away from its nearest competitor.[15]

Although in retrospect, the period saw Torquay develop into one of the major European resorts, these years saw a considerable divergence of opinion within the resort over the path which it should take. The decade prior to 1914 had seen increasing numbers of a different type of visitor in the town, often drawn from the working classes of the northern manufacturing towns on day or weekend trips by rail. This had provoked vociferous condemnation from a powerful interest group of residents in the still genteel resort. Silenced during the war when the tripper trade largely disappeared, this opposition re-emerged in the twenties when there were constant debates concerning the influx of less fashionable visitors into the town. The growth in the numbers of trippers from the Midlands was especially rapid during the twenties and on Bank Holiday Monday in 1928, for instance, over 10,000 trippers arrived in Torquay by train in just two days.[16] An issue which threw this 'social tone' debate into extremely sharp relief in the later twenties was the running of Sunday train excursions to the town. During 1927-8 Torquay Council rejected by seventeen votes to twelve a move to encourage the Sunday trips. The local newspaper, the *Torquay Times*, had opposed the suggestion on Sunday observance grounds and the local Chamber of Commerce opposed it on the grounds that such a move would detract from the social tone of the town.[17]

Certainly the 1920s was a decade of considerable internal strife within Torquay's decision-making circles as various factions sought to dictate the resort's development. There were inherent divisions between those with a vested interest in the holiday industry, such as hoteliers, caterers and motor coach operators, and those who sought to check further expansion in the industry, particularly retired residents. These rifts widened as economic difficulties encouraged the tourism industry to attract a broader range of visitors in an effort to maintain profits. After the slump of 1921 business was especially difficult, as the moderate recovery of 1924-5 was undermined in 1926 by the General Strike, and between 1927 and 1930 the resort experienced only moderate trade. Perhaps the greatest indication of the depth of the division in the resort was the formation of the Citizen's League in 1930. An alliance of those in Torquay who opposed further development of the town's tourist industry, the League was at its most influential during 1931 when it succeeded in gaining three seats on the Borough council.[18]

Ranged against this pressure group were those who favoured further expansion and argued for continued local authority investment in the town's tourism infrastructure. Such arguments were mainly articulated through Torquay's Hoteliers Association and the town's Chamber of Commerce, two organisations which exerted considerable influence over the political landscape during the inter-war years. In 1927 those in favour of developing the holiday industry to attract a broader range of visitors lost the debate over encouraging Sunday train excursions, principally because the pro-tourism lobby was not united on the issue. Overall, throughout the twenties and thirties, however, led by these two powerful trade organisations, they were successful in promoting their ideas. As a result, Torquay continued investing heavily in tourism projects in these years, and crucially, unlike some of its Devon rivals, seized the opportunities at an early stage for further publicity activities presented by the Health and Watering Places Act of 1921. The resort adopted the Act in December 1922 and embarked on a programme of restructuring its committees with tourism remits.[19] In fact, the adoption of this Act in 1922, and the decisive defeat of the anti-tourism lobby which that entailed, proved critical in influencing the path chosen by the resort over the next two decades. During the early- and mid-twenties Torquay increasingly professionalised its resort services' administration, rationalising the committees responsible for tourism direction and employing professional staff to promote the resort, moves which gave the resort a significant edge over its Devon rivals. In 1921 two powerful new committees were set up, a separate Parks and Pleasure Grounds Committee, together with a Baths and Beaches Committee. This move was consolidated three years later when the town's Medical Baths, popular with convalescing visitors and a notable tourist attraction, were transferred to an energetic Baths and Publicity Committee keen to initiate ambitious advertising programmes. When the Baths were again transferred, this time to the Entertainments Committee, the Publicity Committee was then able to concentrate solely on promotional activities and assumed even greater prominence in the Council's structure.[20]

The tangible results of the work of these committees during the twenties and thirties was heavy investment in the town's tourism facilities as Torquay sought to compete with its rivals on the English South Coast and on the French Riviera. For example, the acquisition of open spaces for recreational use emerges as a clear policy of the Torquay Borough Council in these years. This strategy was begun with the purchase of over 100 acres of land from the Ilsham estate in 1919 and continued with the acquisition of six acres at the Abbey Gardens on the seafront the following year. Here, the Council created new bowling greens, two mini-golf courses and seventeen tennis courts, all of which became very popular additions to Torquay's tourist amenities.[21] Perhaps the most significant initiative in this area, however, was the move to secure almost 300 acres in the Cockington Valley between 1928 and 1934. The local authority decided to preserve the old village in its original layout and today the Cockington Court Mansion and the picturesque streets and cottages form valuable tourist attractions in their own right.[22]

This policy of purchasing land for recreational and tourist use was only one aspect of the local authority's concerted programme to develop Torquay into a major resort during this period. Other initiatives included the continued heavy subsidisation of an extensive and varied entertainments programme, particularly the council's controversial support for a morning orchestra at the seafront pavilion despite hefty losses.[23] There was also a considerable investment in the bricks and mortar of tourism facilities. For example, in 1934 the local authority took the Babbacombe Cliff Railway into municipal ownership, purchasing the highly profitable line for £40,000, and the authority also twice refurbished the Torquay Marine Spa, in 1928 and 1935, recognising the Spa's integral role in the resort's reputation as a health centre.[24] Perhaps the most impressive illustration of Torquay Borough Council's commitment to developing the town as a resort, however, was the programme of development begun during 1938-9. This entailed the remodelling of the seafront pavilion, the construction of a concert hall in nearby Babbacombe, and a £100,000 scheme to remodel the town's seafront. This was a remarkable package of capital investment, an ambitious programme intended to provide Torquay with an enviable range of entertainments venues. If the outbreak of World War Two in 1939 had not prevented their completion, these facilities would have made Torquay one of Europe's best equipped seaside resorts.[25]

Torquay's Promotional Activities

As we have seen, during the inter-war years Torquay developed from the fashionable watering place it was in 1900 into one of Europe's most prominent modern resorts. Although this transformation was attributable to the resort's natural attractions, its tourist facilities and the presence in the town of numerous high class hotels, much of Torquay's success was also built on the foundations provided by its image creators. Working in close harmony in the pursuit of common goals, the local authority, the railway companies, and the town's tourism trading interests collaborated in pursuing resort promotion initiatives. In establishing the resort as 'The Queen of the English

Plate 2. Images of a chic 1920s resort. The 1928 guide cover epitomises Torquay's inter-war promotional literature, conveying impressions of an exclusive destination to rival the French Riviera. (Torquay Library)

Riviera', this partnership beguiled would-be visitors with an impression of a resort enjoying mild winters and warm summers, characterised by palm-tree-lined promenades and offering both elegance and luxury (see Plate 2).

As a resort aiming to attract a national and international clientele in a fashionable market, Torquay had long had a relatively sophisticated approach to promotion. Underpinned by considerable financial resources and enjoying an excellent relationship with the Great Western Railway Company, Torquay set high standards in resort promotion, both in the quality of its publicity material and in the organisational framework of its promotional activities. The history of these activities dates to the period before 1900, but it was during 1902-13 that the resort's publicity activities began to assume a modern form, a trend consolidated in the inter-war years.[26]

The Chamber of Commerce, established in 1903, played a vital role in this process, working both independently and in concert with the Torquay Municipal Borough Council. The crucial breakthrough came in 1905-6 with the formation of an advertising fund jointly administered by the Town Council and the Chamber of Commerce, a move described by the 1906 Annual Chamber of Commerce Report as the 'outstanding feature of the year's work'.[27] It is no exaggeration to describe the creation of this Joint Advertising Committee as the most significant administrative innovation in the history of Torquay Council's tourism promotion activities. The Committee was to prove an effective and enduring body, fulfilling a vital co-ordinating role between public and private sectors and forming the corner-stone of Torquay's publicity services for much of the twentieth century. Throughout the operation of the Committee it included representatives of the Hoteliers Association as well as the Chamber of Commerce, recognising the contributions these bodies made to the publicity funds. Indeed, these pressure groups have exerted a great deal of influence over advertising policies during the century. Although their ability to mobilise public opinion behind demands for more advertising varied over the years, broadly speaking they were successful in defeating those factions within the town who opposed tourism development.

Another key factor in the success of the Council's advertising ventures was the good relationship its officers and members developed with the Great Western Railway Company's publicity unit. Although Torquay co-operated in joint advertising initiatives with several railway companies, including the London and North Eastern Railway and the London and South Western Railway, it was the material produced in conjunction with the Great Western which came to epitomise its inter-war publicity efforts. This co-ordinated approach was by no means peculiar to Torquay for resorts throughout Great Britain worked in collaboration with the rail companies, advertising in the national and local press, publishing guides and folders for distribution by the railways, travel agents and the councils' publicity departments, and producing posters for nation-wide display. The Great Western was a vital partner in resort promotion throughout Devon, its help crucial to both Torquay and the other resorts it served. What was different in its relationship with Torquay was the closeness with which the two organisations worked.[28]

The period 1919-39 saw the apogee of the material produced by the Torquay and Great Western partnership. The mid-twenties were the 'Go Great Western' years, when more aggressive publicity began to supplement that backbone of inter-war publicity, the small advertisements which appeared in the same position each week in hundreds of local papers. The replacement in 1924 of the old Great Western advertising department with a new publicity department run by W.H. Fraser marked the beginning of this new era in the history of the Company's publicity activities. Under his direction the promotional activities were to reach their zenith. Between 1924 and 1928 printings of the *Holiday Haunts* brochure doubled to 200,000 and, more importantly as far as Torquay was concerned, Fraser carried through an ambitious programme of joint advertising with resorts whereby the local authorities and the company shared the publicity costs, a campaign which included press as well as poster and folder schemes.[29] This policy of co-operation continued until the early sixties when British Rail (formed in 1947) withdrew from joint advertising, folder production and poster display, announcing that in future seaside resorts would have to provide their own posters for display at stations and pay the railway companies normal commercial rates for the space.[30]

The amount spent by Torquay Council, both in co-operation with the railways and on its own schemes, reflected the town's ambitions as a resort. In 1924 it was advertising both in the South of France and West Africa, illustrating its position as an international resort, whilst in 1925 it spent almost £3,000 on promotion, including £400 for advertisements on London buses, £200 for illuminated signs at Paddington Station and over £1,000 on posters, folders and guides.[31] Although Torquay could not rival the £20,000 annual publicity budget of Blackpool, Britain's greatest resort, the town was a high spender in the Devon context in the late thirties. By the eve of the Second World War, guide and folder numbers had increased so that 80,000 folders were being produced annually with Great Western co-operation, 10,000 of them in French and 10,000 in Dutch. This compared with 10,000 Sidmouth Council guides, financed from a modest publicity budget of only £300, whilst Exmouth, which targetted a broader tourism market, produced 25,000 guides, 1,000 more than Ilfracombe.[32]

It was Torquay's financial resources which gave it the edge over the other Devon resorts. By the early fifties the Torquay Borough Council was allocating between £1,500 and £2,000 a year to advertising alone, rising to £4,000 by the end of the decade, over three times the budget of Ilfracombe's publicity services.[33] Furthermore these municipal campaigns were supplemented by the considerable resources of Torquay's numerous exclusive hotels, all of which were active in promotion. During the inter-war period Torquay was clearly in a different market to the other Devon resorts. Until the later fifties Torquay considered itself in direct competition with the resorts of Southern France, especially Cannes, for the luxury tourism market. As the *Torquay Times* commented in 1928, 'The serious rival to well-known seaside resorts and Torquay in particular, is the Riviera, whose climate and charms are so persistently advocated by posters and pamphlets'.[34] It was the topographical and climatic similarities between the two resorts which enabled Torquay to make the comparison, claims which were taken seriously by contemporary commentators. As *The Times* noted in 1931:

> Torquay is certainly the English equivalent of Cannes. There is no resort which, apart from a certain prim austerity in the administration of the licensing laws, comes nearer in character and amenities to the most progressive of Mediterranean towns.[35]

Conclusion

In the inter-war period the administration of Torquay's tourism activities and particularly its promotional activities developed from amateur and piecemeal origins into an impressive professional organisation. It was these years which laid the foundations for the consolidation of the town's reputation as a major resort after the Second World War. Throughout the inter-war years it is clear that, despite the on-going internal conflicts within Torquay, the town pursued a broad strategy of tourism development with the objective of maintaining its position at the leading edge of Britain's seaside industry. In 1900 all of Devon's resorts were 'select' and 'respectable'.

By 1939 some, particularly Ilfracombe and Exmouth, had developed into 'popular' resorts, whilst others, notably Sidmouth, strove to maintain a genteel atmosphere. Torquay, on the other hand, dominating the county's holiday industry as its largest resort, was unique in sustaining its fashionable image and continuing to appeal to an upper-middle class market whilst also supporting a 'popular' dimension. As a large resort it was able to sustain more than one character and, as early as the late thirties, although more clearly from the fifties, it achieved a 'popular fashionability'. Many of the other Devon resorts were uncertain of their desired image or target market or tried to cultivate more than one and failed.

Torquay successfully repositioned itself in the changing leisure market of the twentieth century by pursuing a *via media* between the selectivity of Sidmouth and the popularity of resorts such as Paignton, Exmouth and Ilfracombe. Its adept responses to the changes in holidaymaking patterns enabled it to maintain its role as Devon's premier resort. Much of its success lay in the resort's favourable geographical position and natural amenities and its effective transport links. Its relationship with the Great Western Railway was particularly important, especially in resort promotion schemes. And not least important, Torquay was able to command greater financial resources than its rivals within Devon. Between 1900 and 1914 the resort invested heavily in its leisure amenities to attract an increasing share of those tourists who were now visiting seaside resorts for entertainment rather than health reasons. During the inter-war period these resources enabled the resort through its own initiatives to widen the gap between itself and the stagnating Ilfracombe, for example, and by the end of the thirties, the range and the quality of Torquay's tourism attractions was unchallenged within Devon.

It was the inter-war period which confirmed Torquay as an international resort. Always one of the United Kingdom's most fashionable resorts, the town nevertheless jettisoned the chimera of exclusivity after some initial hesitancy. In these critical years, the town realigned its image, as for the first time, in the twenties and thirties, Torquay welcomed the influx of lower middle and working class visitors which spelt the end of the resort's 'gentry' era.

Much of the explanation for Torquay's resilience must lie in the activities of its local authority policy-makers and its business community. The commitment of Torquay's local authority, its Hoteliers Association and its Chamber of Commerce provided the resort with the innovative drive and the financial resources which enabled it to remain at the forefront of the British seaside resort industry in this period. There were conflicts between those who opposed further spending on tourism and those who argued that visitor numbers depended on the provision of spacious promenades, gardens and entertainment venues. That Torquay did spend huge sums on such attractions despite the drain on municipal resources demonstrates the resort community's high level of commitment to the promotion of its tourism industry. Such commitment enabled Torquay to be a highly successful and eclectic adopter and adapter of tourism development schemes throughout the inter-war years.

NOTES

1   This paper is drawn from N.J. Morgan, 'Perceptions, Patterns and Policies of Tourism: The Development of the Devon Seaside Resorts During the Twentieth Century with Special Reference to Torquay and Ilfracombe', unpublished University of Exeter PhD thesis, 1991.

2   N. Yates, 'Selling the seaside', *History Today*, XXXVIII (1988), 20-7; J.K. Walton and J. Walvin, eds., *Leisure in Britain, 1780-1939* (Manchester, 1983); S. Jones, *Workers at Play: A Social and Economic History of Leisure, 1918-1939* (1986); J. Walvin, *A Social History of the Popular Seaside Holiday: Beside the Seaside* (1978); and A. Marwick, 'British life and leisure and the First World War', *History Today*, XV (1965), 409-19.

3   Census Reports, 1901-1951, and Devon County Council, *Devon in Figures* (Exeter, 1985).

4   This trend is reflected in a number of newspaper reports at the time, for instance, *The Times*, 2 August 1929, and *Ilfracombe Chronicle*, 24 July and 18 Sept. 1920. See also, T.C. Barker, 'The international history of motor transport', *Journal of Contemporary History*, 20 (1) (1985), 3-19.

5   This development is supported by Yates, 'Selling the seaside', 21.

6   *Torquay Times*, 6 July 1923.

7   J.F. Travis details this development in his, *The Rise of the Devon Seaside Resorts, 1750-1900* (Exeter, 1993).

8   For details of local authority activities see the minutes of Torquay Municipal Borough Council and Sidmouth, Ilfracombe and Exmouth Urban District Councils, 1919-39.

9   See, for instance, this debate in Ilfracombe, *Ilfracombe Chronicle*, 2 May and 20 June 1925.

10   *Western Times*, 27 Jan., 3 and 10 Feb. and 31 March 1939, and also *Western Times*, 17 Feb. and 3 and 17 March 1939.

11   *Ilfracombe Chronicle*, 5 May 1923; Ilfracombe Urban District Council, Minutes, 29 July 1924; and *Ilfracombe Chronicle*, 19 July and 24 Aug. 1924.

12   Nuffield College Social Reconstruction Survey, May 1944, *Devon Tourist Trade*, PRO HLG 82/46.

13   P. Russell, *A History of Torquay and the Famous Anchorage of Torbay* (Torquay, 1960).

14   For details of the Torquay Pavilion see Morgan, 'Perceptions, Patterns and Policies', 290-3.

15   Morgan, 'Perceptions, Patterns, and Policies', 273.

16   *Torquay Times*, 10 Aug. 1928.

17   Torquay Municipal Borough Council, Monthly and Special Committee, 6 May 1927.

18   Morgan, 'Perceptions, Patterns, and Policies', 105; and reports in *Torquay Times*, 26 Sept., 31 Oct. and 7 Nov. 1930, and 23 Jan. 1931.

19   Torquay Municipal Borough Council, Monthly and Special Committee, 5 Dec. 1922.

20   Morgan, 'Perceptions, Patterns, and Policies', chap. 6.

21   Torquay Municipal Borough Council, Special Committee, 18 July 1921 and 31 March 1922; *Torquay Times*, 29 Feb. and 7 March 1924; and Russell, *History of Torquay*, 151.

22   *Torquay Times*, 6 Jan. 1928, 9 Sept. 1932, and 6 Oct. 1933.

23   Nuffield, *Devon Tourist Trade*; and *The Times*, 10 Nov. 1921.

24   *Torquay Times*, 23 July 1926 and 9 March and 8 June 1934; Torquay Municipal Borough Council, Harbour and Baths Committee, 4 July 1927, Finance Committee, 25 July 1927; *Torquay Times*, 22 Feb. 1929; Torquay Municipal Borough Council, Baths Committee, 13 Sept. 1934; and *Torquay Times*, 7 Feb. and 3 July 1936.

25   *Torquay Times*, 29 Jan. 1937 and 7 Oct. and 7 Dec. 1938. See also, Morgan, 'Perceptions, Patterns, and Policies', 309.

26   Morgan, 'Perceptions, Patterns, and Policies', chap.6.

27   Torquay Chamber of Commerce, Annual Report, 1906.

28   Torquay Municipal Borough Council, Publicity Committee, 12 May 1927. See also, R. Burdett Wilson, *Go Great Western: A History of GWR Advertising* (Newton Abbot, 1970), 16.

29   *Ibid.*, 43 and 30.

30   Torquay Municipal Borough Council, Publicity Committee, 12 July 1962.

31   Torquay Municipal Borough Council, Joint Advertising Committee, 15 Jan. 1924.

32   Torquay Municipal Borough Council, Joint Advertising Committee, 1939.
33   *Torquay Times*, 22 Aug. 1952 and 29 May 1953; and Torquay Municipal Borough Council, Joint Advertising Committee, 3 Feb. 1953.
34   *Torquay Times*, editorial, 7 Aug. 1925.
35   *The Times*, 21 Dec. 1931.

THE RISE OF YACHTING IN ENGLAND AND SOUTH DEVON REVISITED, 1640-1827

Janet Cusack

Introduction

The study of leisure, and the activities of leisure time, is now widely accepted as a serious and proper academic interest, with both social and economic aspects. This paper arises from a wider study of the development of 'Aquatics', recreational and competitive rowing and sailing, in England and South Devon over the period 1640-1914.

Yachting – that is the use of sailing boats for pleasure – like any other form of leisure pursuit, varies according to the social and economic characteristics of the society in which its participants live. It can be regarded as an individual activity, giving aesthetic pleasure and physical or psychological challenge, including the opportunity to play out individual fantasies, such as realistic war games. It can also be considered as a means of asserting or claiming high social or economic status by conspicuous consumption, as suggested by Thorstein Veblen.[1] Leisure pursuits also constitute economic activities. For instance, yachting requires capital expenditure on the purchase of a vessel, and further regular expenditure on maintenance. Direct employment is and was produced among crews, boatyard employees and club servants, while the sponsorship, service and exploitation of regattas and races also provide economic opportunities for entrepreneurial individuals and groups.

The history of yachting has a sparse scholarly literature. Probably the best general works available are Arthur Clark, *The History of Yachting: 1600-1815* (1904), and *British Yachts and Yachtsmen: A Complete History of British Yachting from the Middle of the Sixteenth Century to the Present Day* (1907). There are some club histories, including those of the Royal Thames Yacht Club and the Royal Yacht Squadron. The literature covering developments in Devon before 1825 is even more limited, being virtually the first few pages of the histories of the Teignmouth and Torquay regattas.[2] This paucity of literature has meant that most of the work for this paper has very largely been based upon original sources.

A brief statement of the traditional popular view of the history of English yachting is that the socially exclusive sport of yacht racing was brought to England from Holland by Charles II in 1660, lapsed after the fall of James II, and was revived on the safe waters of the Thames during the late eighteenth and early nineteenth centuries. It is further thought that in 1815, at the end of the Napoleonic Wars, some yachting was transferred to the Channel at Cowes, with the foundation of the Royal Yacht Squadron, and that, with the sea clear of privateer activity, a culture of yacht cruising and racing could then spread from Cowes through English waters and beyond.

This paper will, first, examine the traditional view of the national history of pleasure sailing and yachting, the development of yacht racing upon the Thames, and the establishment of the Royal Yacht Squadron at Cowes. It will then consider the parallel development of yachting upon the South Devon coast in the eighteenth and early nineteenth centuries.

The Early Development of English Yachting

Pleasure boating on a small scale in England did not begin in 1660. Medieval illuminated manuscripts show pleasant aquatic picnics, the boat being well supplied with company, music, and wine.[3] Most pioneer aquatic recreation, for obvious reasons of proximity, comfort and safety, was confined to inland waters, but a few amateur watermen made coastal voyages. Possibly the earliest small-boat pleasure voyage recorded in detail was that of Richard Ferris, who wagered in 1590 that English command of the Channel was such that a wherry could make a safe passage from London to Bristol. Ferris recruited a friend, and wisely, since he was 'never trayned up to the water', a Thames waterman. The party used a purpose-built wherry, and the passage was made by easy stages, a procedure justified by Ferris: 'Sometimes we were constrained to put into these places for want of victuals, sometime for to have their certificates to testify of our being there: sometimes we were weather bound ... and our welcome in all places deserveth due commendations'. They were certainly well entertained. In Devon the crew visited Dartmouth for two days, and enjoyed 'good entertainment and great courtesie ... by the inhabitants'. They were entertained at Sower Cove by Sir William Courtenay, 'a verie bountiful knight', then sailed to Plymouth to lavish naval hospitality. The voyage ended at Bristol on 2 August, with a civic reception, 'where we were feasted most royally'. The social nature of the excursion is emphasised by the fact that the wherry left London on Midsummer Day, and only twenty-four of the next forty days were spent at sea.[4]

Since 1643 some English pleasure boats have been known as yachts. *Falconer's Marine Dictionary* of 1780 gave three definitions of the term: 'Vessels of state, usually employed to convey princes, ambassadors or other great personages', less elaborate vessels used by commissioners of the excise, navy and customs, and yachts 'used as pleasure vessels by private gentlemen.'[5] The 1935 definition given by the *Oxford English Dictionary* included both the official and pleasure concept: 'A light, fast-sailing ship, in early use especially for the conveyance of royal or other important persons; later a vessel, usually light and comparatively small, propelled by motive power other than oars, and used for pleasure excursions, cruising, etc., and now especially one built and rigged for racing.'[6]

As stated above, there is a traditional belief that the practice of pleasure sailing and the word 'yacht' were introduced into England by Charles II on his return from exile in Holland. It is true that the word 'yacht' only passed into common use after the Restoration. Sir William Lower in his description of the return of Charles II in 1660 thought it necessary to define the term: '[Yachts] a kind of little frigats, whereof persons of condition make use upon the rivers, in passing from one province to another, for necessity, or for diversion.'[7] John Evelyn also noted the new word: 'I sail'd this morning with His Majesty in one of his yachts (or pleasure boats), vessels not known among us.'[8] The word was, however, in limited use in England before 1660. The *Oxford English Dictionary* quotes the use of the words 'yeaghes', 'yoathes' and 'yaughts' in 1557, 1613 and 1616, but in these cases the writers were describing Norwegian or Dutch boats. A later example cited by the *Dictionary*, of Richard Johnson, *King and Commonwealth* (1630), suggests the use of the word for a pleasure vessel, since the extract mentions the 'Emperor, who yet had never greater vessel than a Punt or Yough upon the Danuby'.[9] The use of 'yough', 'yought', 'yaught', 'yacht', to describe a specific English vessel, was noted by T. Barrett Leonard in 1905 to be included in accounts at Herstmonceaux Castle covering the period 1643-69.[10] Further reference to Mr Barrett Leonard's sources has provided more details of the yacht.

Francis, Lord Dacre, owner of Herstmonceaux and Pevensey in 1643, was described in his family history as having: 'Great delight in all manners relating to navigation ... he had a vessel of his own ... in which he use to make excursions'.[11] The household account book of Herstmonceaux Castle for the years 1643-69 provides considerable details of the expenditure on the pleasure boat. No costs were given for the building of the yacht, as she was obviously in commission when the account started in September 1643, £1 being paid for 'tow and nails used about my Lords yough at Pemsie', with '2 pieces of beefe, 2 joynts of mutton, one joynt of veale, a cople of chickens was sent to my Lords yough at Pemsie'. The yacht was indeed well provisioned. In June 1645 the steward sent to sea '4 stone of beefe, 2 stone of bakan, 2 joints of mutton, 1 barrell of beere, 3 bottles of wine'. John Nichouls was paid as 'keeper of my Lords yought' in November 1643, at a rate of £3.10 for '7 weekes wages and dyett', but by 1644 Thomas Gawen was in charge of maintenance.

The size of Lord Dacre's yacht was not stated, but some clues may be obtained from details of work done and spares purchased. A dock was built for her in 1643, and in October and November of the same year repair work was done on the vessel, probably as a part of laying-up. Mr Wright was paid 15s.3d. for 'mending and trimming the yaught' on 21 October, while another billing of 28 October was for '3 li of Oakum, 100 3^d nails, 200 scupper nails, for a shiver for the mast, beere for workmen for ye shipcarpenters work, 6 daies for 2 labourers for digging under ye yacht & helping to house the sailes, £1.6.7'. A 113lb anchor was purchased in November 1643, and a 36lb anchor in April 1644. The anchor sizes, combined with the fact that no more than two crewmen were ever paid at the same date, suggest that the vessel was probably no larger than 10 tons. Use of the yacht did not follow a regular summer season pattern. In 1644 on 30th March the pilot John Waters was paid £2.10 for 'conducting my Lords yough from Grauesend to Herstmonceaux', and canvas for sails was purchased in the following May. By 27 July, however, the boat was laid up: 'paid for the labourers helping to unrig my Lords yaught 5s', chandlery bills were paid, and crew paid 'for attending at Pemsie to go with my Lord's yought'. After 1644 the accounts rarely mention the yacht, which probably reflects Dacre's increasing Civil War involvement, or may be linked to the fact that other account book entries show a huge increase in taxation.[12]

Pleasure sailing took place in the English Royal Family well before 1660. According to his autobiography, Phineas Pett was ordered in 1604: 'To build a little vessel for the young prince Henry to disport himself in above London Bridge, and to aquaint his Grace with shipping and the manner of that element.' The 25-foot *Disdain* was 'garnished with painting and carving both within board and without', and supplied with 'ordnance and powder from the Tower'. This vessel could be dismissed as an expensive educational aid for a royal child, but the Prince, as a young adult in 1612, ordered a pleasure boat for Channel sailing: 'A small new ship, which was to be as a pinnace to the great ship, the *Prince*, in which the Prince's Highness did purpose to solace himself sometimes into the narrow seas.' Sadly, Prince Henry died before his boat was ready.[13]

The practical pleasure sailing of Henry's nephew, Charles II, certainly pre-dated his Dutch exile. As the *British Yachts and Yachtsmen* of 1907 declares, when he was in Jersey in 1646 a sympathiser provided a pleasure boat, 'beautifully appointed, built for him at St Malo; she had 12 pairs of oars and two masts', and Charles was reported as sailing her around the Channel Islands.[14] However, yachting as an important Court activity did begin with the Restoration in 1660, and early boats were strongly influenced by Dutch designs. King Charles had over twenty yachts built and, incidentally, set a precedent for future yachtsmen in that he managed to have most of them financed by a business account. Indeed, Samuel Pepys seemed surprised when he heard that the king was about to pay for one of his own vessels: '[The king] talking of building a new yacht, which the king is resolved to have built out of his private purse, he having some contrivance of his own.'[15] Charles II, like his brother, the Duke of York, was a yachting enthusiast: he cruised and raced his own vessels, one race for 100 guineas being recorded by John Evelyn in 1661.[16] Charles took a keen interest in his boats, rising at 5 a.m. to inspect yachts on the stocks, and to try out new vessels, as when Pepys noted: 'We were overtaken by the king in his barge, he having been down the River with his yacht this day, for pleasure to try it.'[17] Charles' interest in his yachts was commented upon by Henry Saville in 1689, when sent to Calais to trace an overdue vessel. He wrote to a friend that any delay in tracing the yacht 'may perhaps be irksome to our princes, whose favourites next to their dogs their yachts are'.[18]

The conventional view of King Charles II as the father of English yachting, however, should be treated with caution, since most of his yachts were naval vessels used for government business, and were rightly charged to the Admiralty. *Bezan* was used by Pepys in September 1665; 'the King's pleasure boats' brought 'the Dunkirke money, being 400,000 pistolls' from Calais in 1662,[19] and a royal yacht was lent to Captain Collins for his British coastal survey.[20] Captain Collins' survey was a complement to an intensive basic research programme, intended to produce practical results for seafarers, which was carried out by the newly formed Royal Society, and reported in early issues of the *Philosophical Transactions*. The records of the Royal Society make clear that the research included the design of programmes for collection of data worldwide by seamen and studies of astronomy (with associated instrumentation); the properties of air, with direct relation to weather studies; the effects of changes of temperature upon the human body; magnetic studies, linked with compass design; investigations of salinity, and density studies; while at the same time basic mathematical techniques were developed so that data could be analysed.[21] Theoretical work was combined with a series of practical developments of navigational techniques and ship design, and royal yachts under Charles and his successors were test models for maritime research. This ranged from major problems, such as hull design, to smaller innovations: '[His Majesty] talked to me of a new varnish for ships instead of pitch, ... and of the gilding with which his new yacht was beautified'.[22] Possibly because of this function British royal yachts gained a reputation for excellence of construction and when the *Catherine*, a 'very costly yacht of His Majesty the King of England', was captured by the Dutch and taken into Amsterdam in 1673, she aroused great interest and was given a thorough technical examination.[23]

It is probable that the real contribution of Charles II and James II to the development of English pleasure sailing and yacht racing was that their personal enthusiasm set a fashion for the possession of private yachts which survived the fall of the Stuart monarchy. Most early yacht owners had Court connections. In 1663, as Clark has shown, Sir William Batten owned the *Charlotte*, claimed to be 'the first private yacht to be built in England',[24] and the Duke of Richmond consulted Pepys about his yacht in late 1668, paying for the consultation with the gift of a doe from Cobham. In 1665 Pepys used a yacht owned by Mr Ashburnham and Colonel Wyndham on urgent business for the king on a passage from Erith to Queenborough.[25] Pepys described Colonel Wyndham as 'the only gentleman of estate that was ever known to addict himself to the sea only for his pleasure in any age, having never been in any service at sea, either merchant or the King's, but only do what he has done for pleasure and from his own natural addiction'.[26] Colonel Wyndham was followed by other enthusiasts so that during the late seventeenth and early eighteenth centuries there was a slow but steady increase in the use of private pleasure boats.

The eighteenth and early nineteenth centuries were a time of quiet national development in yacht cruising and transport on English coastal and inland waters, and on more distant voyages. Yachts continued to be used for the transport of royal personages. Stephen Fisher has recently reminded us of the three journeys made by George I from the Thames to Holland and Hanover, in 1723, 1725 and 1727. In 1723 King George, sent on his way with 'the repeated huzzas of his loyal subjects', gun salutes and 'extraordinary fireworks and illuminations', embarked on the *Carolina* yacht at Greenwich, and sailed with a fair wind to Helvoet-slys, where he transferred to a Dutch yacht for the passage to Vaart, and thence travelled by road to Hanover. The same yacht and route were used in 1725, when the Channel crossing was made in foul weather, and a crossing was made again in 1727.[27] Evidence of a general interest in yachting is provided by the fact that some eighteenth-century technical works carried plans of yachts. F.A. Dingley has pointed to the pictures of a 'yacht sloop' given in the manuscript 'Gwyn's Book of Ships', dated c.1769,[28] while David Macgregor has noted that plans of yachts, sloops and cutters appeared in Marmaduke Stalkartt's *Naval Architecture*, published in London in 1781.[29] Some private estates had small fleets of pleasure boats. Arthur Young in 1768, at Luton Hoo, the estate of the Earl of Bute, noted a lake equipped with two pleasure boats and a sloop with flying colours.[30] Yachting not surprisingly also spread to the colonies. Arthur Clark in his work of 1904 described an engraving of 1717 which showed Colonel Morris' *Fancy* of New York.[31] By 1750 yachting was established both in England and abroad. The journal of the naval officer Augustus Hervey shows that he was very well acquainted with social maritime recreation. He described the year September 1752 to September 1753, when he commanded the *Phoenix* in the Mediterranean, spending his commission ferrying money and important passengers, interspersed with an energetic social life, as 'a year's yachting'. In 1748 and 1753 he organised aquatic entertainments on the canals at Leghorn, and while in Portugal sailed in the yachts belonging to Don João de Bomposto, nephew of the king of Portugal. Hervey's yachting covered a wide range of activities, from dubious social visits, 'I often went sailing up the river with Don João ... and to nunneries', to intelligence gathering among a French group of nine men of war that entered Lisbon in 1755.[32]

The motivation of early English yachtsmen was varied. A display of wealth was implicit in the ownership of costly and spectacular private vessels. Some used sailing to play out fantasies. The three-week holiday voyage of Lord Orford in the Fens, in 1774, was recorded in three journals. Mr Thomas Roberts, 'Volunteer on board the Fleet', wrote in naval style, referring to Orford as 'the Admiral', commanding a 'fleet ... cruising in the narrow Seas of Cambridgeshire, Lincolnshire, Northamptonshire, Huntingdonshire, and of Norfolk and Suffolk'. Mr Farrington and Lord Orford himself, wrote in the style of explorers traversing unknown seas, and a classical element was introduced by small craft racing carried out along the way with boats named after those used in a regatta recorded in the *Aeneid*.[33] Lord Orford's party were not the only yachtsmen to use yachts to play at war, a practice which continued into the nineteenth century. Much of the ritual and practice of yachting, the heavy armament of yachts; naval manoeuvres under a commodore; cruising in fleet formation; and visits of yachtsmen as sightseers to overseas wars, or even active intervention in military disputes, suggests that, for many yachtsmen, their hobby was a combination of aristocratic display and elaborate, realistic, or even real, war games.

Some early yachtsmen, however, were clearly motivated by a simple pleasure in sailing. Their boats did not suggest conspicuous consumption, and their activities provoked reactions which could not be described as emulation. The lawyer Roger North, for example, cruised the Thames and South Coast in 1687 in a 10-ton yacht, and his autobiography shows great enjoyment, but little display, in his yachting. By North's own description the boat was badly maintained (once sinking on a sandbank under a party of guests), and unseaworthy: 'She was no good sea boat, because she was open aft and might ship a sea and sink her – but in the river she would sail tolerably and work extraordinarily well.' The inhabitants of Harwich thought the yacht unsafe: 'We were asked if we had left our souls in London, because we took so little care of our bodies.' North described sailing as 'one of my mathematical entertainments, for the working of a vessel, its rigging, and position of the sails, do exercise as much of mechanics, as all the other arts of the world'. He never included navigation in his mathematical entertainment, and took a pilot when he left the Thames, but obviously took great pleasure in simply being at sea:

> I, with my friend Mr Chute, sat before the mast in the hatchway, with perspectives and books, the magazine of provisions, and a boy to make a fire and help broil, make tea, chocolate, etc. And thus, passing alternately from one entertainment to another we passed eight whole hours, and scarce knew what time was past. For the day proved cool, the gale brisk, air clear, and no inconvenience to molest us, nor wants to trouble our thoughts, neither business to importune, nor formalities to tease us; so that we came nearer to a perfection of life there than I was ever sensible of otherwise.[34]

Roger North's contemporary, the London mariner and merchant, Thomas Bowery, used his 'yaut', the 14-ton *Duck*, for pleasure and profit. Bowery cruised the Thames estuary extensively in the years

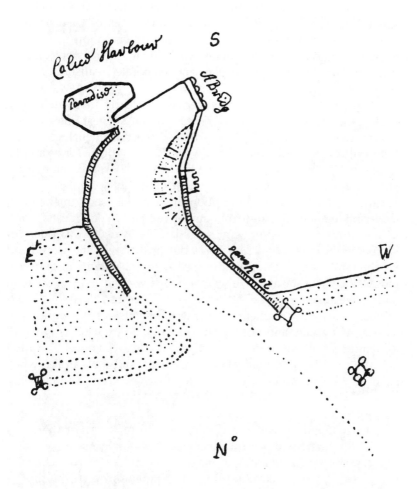

Figure 1. The entrance to Calais, sketched by Thomas Bowery on board the yacht *Duck*, 1694. Source: R. C. Temple, ed., *The Papers of Thomas Bowery* (1927), 12.

Plate 1. The brig, John, in Leith Harbour, 1789. Source: J. H. Adeane, ed., The Early Married Life of Maria Josepha, Lady Stanley: with Extracts from Sir John Stanley, Praeterita (1900), 56-60.

between 1694 and 1701, and left a sea-stained notebook of sailing directions, illustrated by sketches, for the creeks and harbours in his cruising area, eighteen of which described the Essex coast and four the Kent coast. In 1694 Bowery and a fellow merchant enjoyed an expenses-shared cruising holiday by yacht and public canal boat in the Low Countries. The sketch which Bowery made of the entrance to Calais on this excursion is shown as Figure 1. Thomas Bowery managed to have his yachting at low cost. The hull of the *Duck*, built at Wapping in 1690, cost £90. There is, unfortunately, no record of the rigging and other fitting-out charges. The owner's accounts show maintenance expenditure of £47.9s.9¾d. between 1690 and 1707, and Bowery's share of the expenses of the Dutch expedition in 1698 was £32.3s.4½d. The *Duck* was sold in March 1707 for £65.16s. However, Bowery chartered his yacht at the rate of £1 per day, earning £2 'for letting out the yacht' in 1704, and a massive £109 in 1705-6 for 109 days hire to the Marquis of Carmarthen. His recorded outlay and income from the yacht thus shows a profit of £7 over 17 years, and while there were doubtless other unrecorded expenses, including the cost of the original fitting out, Thomas Bowery appears to have had a good bargain in his *Duck* 'yaut'.[35]

Yachtsmen and cruising oarsmen, especially in remote areas, were rare, their motivation was not understood, and they were often met with suspicion. For instance, Roger North was subjected to constant searching by Custom-House smacks. Suspicions of piracy arose with a later yachtsman. The journal of John Stanley, aged 23, of Edinburgh, described a pleasure trip to Iceland in 1789. Mr Stanley chartered the brig *John*, (see Plate 1), complete with captain and crew for his yachting voyage, at the reluctant expense of his father. The elder Mr Stanley had thought when the project was first suggested, 'no more seriously of it than a yacht trip to the Hebrides. When he found I was in earnest, he made some objections, but I soon wrung from him his not very slow leave'. His father's attitude is interesting, as it suggests that a yacht excursion in the Hebrides was not, at the time, a remarkable undertaking. The *John* called in at Orkney, then at the Faroe Islands. The Faroese greeted the two-gun brig with caution. 'The first questions asked ... when they came aboard were, whether our was a king's ship, a privateer or a merchantman; and when told we were none of these things, but a yacht coming to these islands merely for the pleasure of seeing them, they seemed to think we were making fools of them.'[36]

Some observers of yachting were simply puzzled. Admiral Sir Byam Martin as a midshipman in about 1800, was in charge of a ship's boat which rescued the crew of a sloop yacht dismasted in the

Channel. The yacht passengers included a 'lady in a black hat', who expressed her gratitude by kissing the midshipman before the assembled ship's company. In a letter home he described his embarrassment and added that he 'could not understand where the *pleasure* of sailing came in, nor why people should call their yachts *pleasure* boats', as he himself was always a victim of sea-sickness.[37]

In addition to the voyages mentioned above, some cruising under sail, although rare, took place in British waters, the Channel, and further afield, much of it doubtless unrecorded. Among the known excursions is that of Mr Smith of Battersea, who took his yacht *Lovely Mary*, originally owned by Mr Clarke of Christchurch, to Margate and Rochester in 1768; while in 1773 Earl Ferrers used a Channel cruise to test an experimental rig, and the Duke of Argyle cruised his yacht the *Princess Augusta* (90 tons) on the Clyde between 1751 and 1755. The Duke of Richmond made frequent pleasure trips to France in a yacht built at Southampton in 1783, and Lord and Lady Craven, in the first peace of 1814, took their three children on a family cruise.[38] Also at least two yachtsmen used their vessels to fetch wine supplies. Lord Courtenay of Powderham Castle, on the Exe estuary, sailed the *Dolphin* to the Channel Islands in 1790, while Mr Taylor of London took the *Cumberland* to Bordeaux in 1791.[39] Although enemy privateers were in the Channel during wartime, few yachts became casualties. The *Hawke* in 1777 was chased into neutral Calais by a French privateer, while the *Zephyr* was reported to have been 'very nearly captured by a French Privateer' when she went outside the Needles in 1800.[40] The Cornish yacht *Bagatelle* of Penzance, however, was sunk in 1808 by the Irish brig *Venus*, which suspected that the yacht was a French privateer. The *Venus* made signals requesting that she identify herself, then opened fire when the owners of *Bagatelle*, ignorant of the signal code, not only failed to provide identification, but continued to approach.[41] Some yachtsmen used South Coast waters for day-cruising, as when in 1782 Lord Torrington enjoyed a day at Weymouth: '[I] took a sail round the harbour's mouth and towards ... Portland ... we attempted fishing, catching only four mackerel ... we landed cold and contented.'[42] The *Hampshire Courier* in 1815 reported an elaborate excursion from Cowes, when several yachts sailed to Netley Abbey, 'with colours flying, and an excellent band of music playing ... which had a very pleasing effect'.[43]

We also have evidence of some deep-water yacht voyages from English ports, for the longer period 1671-1817. There were at least three Atlantic yacht crossings. According to Arthur Clark, the first English transatlantic yacht voyage was that carried out by George Fox and a group of friends, who stayed for some months in Maryland, in

1671-3. This excursion used the yacht *Industry*, a vessel described as 'a very swift sailer'. She leaked, however, and kept both sailors and passengers at the pumps day and night on the return journey. A less sober voyage, a hundred years later, was that of Mr Shuttleham, who took his ten-gun yacht *Lively* (140 tons), with a crew of twenty five and 'a beautiful French woman', from London to Florida in 1784, and then cruised the American coast to Hudson Bay.[44] Also, it is believed that Lord Courtenay, obliged to leave England in haste, sailed the *Dolphin* to New York in 1811, took up residence, and sold his yacht there.[45] At least two long-distance voyages were taken in European waters. In 1775 Edward Weld of Lulworth Castle took a yacht to Portugal, but little is known of the voyage.[46] Another trip to Portugal is better documented. Sir William Curtis, ex-Lord Mayor of London, went to Portugal to see the War in 1809. Sir William's yacht was claimed to be 'the finest pleasure vessel belonging to any British subject', and maintained at a cost of £1,600 a year. He obtained Admiralty permission for the trip with considerable difficulty, and on condition that 'the wealthy Alderman would consent to put his vessel under their [Admiralty] orders'. Sir William 'immediately began to perform his naval duties by storing his vessel with every kind of viands, substantial or luxurious, and abundance of the finest wines. The Marquess of Huntley, and other general officers, readily accepted his hospitable offers to entertain them on their passage'.[47] In 1815 Sir William visited St Petersburg.[48]

Further evidence that early pleasure sailing was not restricted to London, and also that recreational sailing in England in the late eighteenth and early nineteenth centuries was not restricted to the wealthy, is provided by contemporary newspaper reports of accidents. Newspaper reports, then as now, concentrated on the rich and on spectacular events, but they were eager to report accidents, particularly if fatal. Although only a small percentage of aquatic excursions ended in disaster, and the great majority of cruises went unreported, these accident reports can be used to give an indication of the geographical and social range of pleasure sailing. Table 1 gives a sample of these reported English yachting accidents.

Table 1
Some English Yachting Accidents, 1798-1813

Date	Place	Casualties	People Involved
1798	Oxford	3 dead	3 printer's apprentices, master's nephew.
1802	Oxford	3 dead	Mr Mangay and 3 young ladies.
1805	Thames	1 dead	Mr Foote, banker, and sister.
1805	Ramsgate	3 dead	10 persons, including pilot, mayor's daughter, banker's son.
1807	Humber	3 dead	3 young men of Hull.
1807	R. Nene	2 dead	'2 respectable young men of Peterborough, and two other young men'.
1807	Swansea	7 dead	11 persons, junior officers, Custom House clerk, merchant's clerk, surgeon's son.
1807	Longleat	1 dead	Mr Wade, principal artificer at Longleat, 1 mariner, a labourer and his son.
1807	Ambleside	1 dead	Surgeon.
1808	Putney	2 dead	Journeyman and two apprentices.
1810	Parkgate	5 dead	'Eight persons', upset in 'injudicious tack'.
1812	Thames	9 dead	11 married men in a sailing wherry.
1813	Erith	5 dead	6 persons, pin-maker's son and daughter.

Sources: *Gentleman's Magazine*, 1798-1813; *The Times*, 1812-13.[49]

The table shows that there was a wide social spectrum of participants in aquatic recreation in this period, ranging from bankers, surgeons and military officers to journeymen, apprentices, an artificer and a labourer, and that they came from various parts of England and Wales. It is noteworthy that not only was sailing available to people in a range of professions and trades, but that women also participated. They may have been more likely to drown, presumably from a combination of bulky clothing and the fact that few women could swim, although Miss Foote, in 1805, was lucky, as her clothes bore her up whereas her brother sank. It is also evident that some women sailed in small boats when in an advanced state of pregnancy, as certain of the female deaths were ascribed to premature birth rather than drowning, as in the case of the Ramsgate incident of 1805.[50]

The Rise of Competitive Yachting on the Thames

As has been shown, eighteenth- and early nineteenth-century yacht cruising was not confined to the Thames. London became, however, an important yachting centre, and the focus of social yachting, in the form both of club formation and racing under sail. The development of clubs and racing could not take place unless sufficient yacht owners were concentrated in a limited area, which in its turn depended upon the existence of a concentration of wealthy families near suitable water. This situation developed on the Thames in the mid-eighteenth century, as the fashion grew among city families of purchasing a country river-side house, often with a skiff or small yacht moored at the bottom of the garden. The memoirs of William Hickey, a member of one such family in the mid-eighteenth century, detail a yachtsman's progress, from childhood escapades in the family boat, to personal ownership of a small wherry, a sailing skiff, and finally 'a half decked vessel with boom and gaff main sail, fore sail and jib'. Hickey also described other owners, including Mr Smith of Battersea, owner and helmsman of the *Lovely Mary*, a liveryman of the Stationer's Company, with a town house in Leadenhall Street. A legacy of £2,000 a year enabled him to purchase 'a noble house on the border of the river, a little above the town of Battersea', where he lived 'in the true style of old English hospitality, in the midst of a happy family'. Mr Smith was a dissenter and kept strict Sunday observance.[51]

When a sufficiently large population of yachts had accumulated on the Thames some owners began to race. The progress of this racing has been described by Arthur Clark and Douglas Phillips-Birt, and these accounts have been supplemented below by accounts from personal journals, contemporary newspaper accounts, and race sheets in the archives of the Royal Thames Yacht Club. Convincing evidence that a large number of yachts were based on the Thames by 1849 is that when the Prince of Wales gave a cup for a yacht race from Greenwich round the Nore, twelve boats were able and their owners willing to compete in a twenty-four hour race. It was reported that 'the river during the race [was] overspread with sailing yachts, galleys, and small boats'.[52]

Informal racing took place on the Thames among groups of private gentlemen over the next three decades, and in 1775 the Duke of Cumberland gave a cup for a yacht race from Westminster Bridge to Putney Bridge and back, and continued to present an annual cup until 1782.[53] From 1786 to the nineteenth century frequent yacht races took place on the Thames for cups and other prizes financed by commercial sponsors, private individuals, clubs and group subscriptions.

In the mid- and late-eighteenth century many London yachtsmen organised themselves into clubs, usually based in taverns. This was probably an inevitable development for a Thames sport, as clubs were common among Londoners of all classes. The silversmith Brasbridge, who set up in London in 1770, and published his memoirs in 1824, listed the clubs of his youth as: 'the Highflyer Club held at the Turf coffee-house ... the card club at the Crown and Rolls in Chancery Lane ... a sixpenny card club at the Queen's Arms in St Paul's Churchyard ... the Free and Easy under the Rose'.[54] It was therefore to be expected that groups of gentlemen engaged in yachting would meet to dine before or after the activity. William Hickey joined a sailing club which 'dined together once a week at the Swan Tavern, Chelsea', sometime before 1773, where the members subscribed for a silver cup for racing their boats on 'the anniversary of the establishment', and noted that this pattern was repeated up and down the river.[55] Another group met at Battersea. The *Public Advertiser*, when discussing arrangements for the rowing Regatta of 1775, pointed out that: 'several very respectable gentlemen, proprietors of sailing vessels and pleasure boats on the River, held their annual meeting at Battersea'. At this meeting the group decided that 'on the day of the Regatta they would draw their boats up in a line opposite Ranelagh Gardens so as not to be in the way of the competing boats'.[56] One such group in 1775 came to the attention of the Duke of Cumberland, obtained his patronage and adopted the title of the Cumberland Fleet (later the Royal Thames Yacht Club). The Fleet, sailing cutters ranging from four to seventeen tons, became the most highly organised club on the river, with a properly constituted code of sailing rules. Thames clubs had a model on which to base the aquatic aspects of their activities in the form of the oldest yacht club in the British Isles (and, indeed, probably in the world), the Cork Water Club, founded in 1720. Cork members regularly put to sea to parade 'in a number of little vessels which for painting and gilding exceed the king's yacht at Greenwich'. The club rules provided for sailing, signals, dress and conduct, including the very sensible regulation that 'any member as shall talk of sailing after dinner, be fined a bumper'.[57]

Thames sailing clubs provided their members with pleasure, conviviality, some competition, and opportunities for personal and group display. Racing was one form of club activity, but its importance should not be overestimated. It is tempting to gauge the development of yachting by consideration of surviving racing records, but in fact the racing available to yacht owners in the late eighteenth and early nineteenth centuries was very limited, and many yacht owners, in any case, preferred other forms of sailing. The Cumberland Fleet, like the Cork Water Club, spent time in naval manoeuvres and official display. In 1776 members went up the Thames with 'colours flying and music playing', in honour of the king's birthday, and in 1778 the Duke held a formal review of his fleet at Sheerness.[58] Manoeuvres were considered to be so important that signal books were produced in 1779 and 1793 to enable the Commodore to control his vessels. The tradition of sailing in company was long-lasting. The 1827 rules (rule no. 7) of the Thames Yacht Club stated that once a year: 'It will be expected that those members who have boats will sail down the River together, after which, to add to the conviviality of the day, it will be desirable that members who can make it convenient shall dine together.'[59]

Analysis of entries to early Thames races supports the view that in the study of yachting history the significance of racing should not be overemphasised, as even on the Thames, where yacht racing was promoted as a growing sport, most yachts raced infrequently. An analysis of the number of entries to yacht races, including wager contests, sailed on the Thames between 1786-1809, as recorded by surviving race sheets and newspaper reports, shows that, even allowing for a change of ownership of some yachts, racing was a rare event for most yachtsmen, since 46 vessels sailed only one race, 11 only two, and 4 only three. There were some exceptions; the *Mercury*, owned by Mr Astley of the Cumberland Fleet, raced at least nine times, and usually gained a first or second place. Commodore Taylor of the Cumberland Fleet was a regular competitor and consistent winner, taking the Cumberland Cup in 1776, 1780 and again in 1781, and the Vauxhall Cup in 1789.[60] These figures can only be claimed to be approximate, as press reports were not always complete, some races were not reported if news space was in demand, and even if races were reported information was often incomplete. For instance, in 1791 *The Times*, in reporting the Vauxhall Cup Race, mentioned that there were twelve starters, but only gave the names of the first and second boats, while in 1788 *The Times* reported on the same race without mentioning the sailing, but described the subsequent festivities in Vauxhall Gardens.[61]

However, although racing was only a minority interest for many yachtsmen, it became, alongside competitive rowing, a popular spectator sport on the Thames in the period between 1775 and 1827, and hence an important economic activity which attracted commercial sponsors following the original royal patrons. The major sponsors on the Thames were the Pleasure Gardens. Vauxhall Gardens sponsored races for the Cumberland Fleet, when the Duke's seven-year cup run ended, while Astley's Amphitheatre gave an annual cup for yachtsmen, the race being held on the king's birthday, which gave an excuse for a patriotic spectacular at the Amphitheatre in the evening. Newspaper advertisements of races make it very clear these were intended to be curtain-raisers to the evening entertainment at the Gardens or Amphitheatre.[62] Some cheaper publicity was obtained by assistance at, rather than complete sponsorship of, sailing events. For instance, at the Vauxhall Sailing Race in 1805, 'one of the Royal Exchange Assurance boats was fitted up for the Vauxhall Band', and another insurance company gained publicity in 1829 when the starting boat at the Coronation Fleet Race 'was rowed by four of the men belonging to the Palladium Fire Office, in their full dresses, they having tendered their services for the occasion'.[63]

Early yacht clubs were helped by commercial interests, often within their own ranks. For example, the first Commodore of the Cumberland Fleet, Mr Smith, is thought to have been the proprietor of Smith's Pleasure Gardens. This was a small pleasure park occupying about one and a half acres on the south bank of the Thames, immediately south of Vauxhall Bridge. It was often used by visitors to Vauxhall while waiting for the main gardens to open, or by those seeking a quiet supper away from the larger garden. Smith's Pleasure Gardens was used as a base for the Cumberland Fleet. The next owner, Luke Reilly, who took over the Gardens in 1784 changed the name to Cumberland Gardens, and in 1796 donated a silver cup for yacht racing. The Cumberland Fleet used the Gardens as a signal station, had a finishing line between the gardens and a moored boat, and fired cannons from the shore. Races finished there until 1825, when the gardens closed after a fire. Yacht racing brought considerable custom, typical of which was a day in 1824, when a wager race between the *Don Giovanni* and the *Spitfire*, finished at Cumberland Gardens where the cup was 'given to Captain Davey amidst the discharge of calivers and the shouts of a vast crowd of spectators'.[64]

Boatbuilders had an obvious commercial interest in yacht racing, as did watermen, who stood to gain from the business generated by race spectators. Newspapers also gained revenue from race advertisements, and increased circulation from reports and pre-race betting tips. Newspapers supplied sponsors with publicity and gamblers with information on contestants. For instance, in 1792 *The Times* discussed a proposed wager race between the yachts *Phoenix* and *Troliopus*, and noted that current bets were five to four in favour of the *Phoenix*. Also *Bell's Life in London* discussed contestants in 1824: 'The *Fortitude* is a washing tub looking affair, [she] can therefore do little if it blow hard, but while she can carry full sail ... she goes through the water at a surprising rate ... her owners, considering the goodness of their boat, are somewhat deficient in spirit'; '*Venus*, hatch boat, the swiftest below London Bridge, but not calculated for the higher part of the Thames'; '*Mentor*, formerly a good sailer, but now old'.[65] All races gave opportunities for betting, and wager matches not only carried the agreed amounts staked by participants or sponsors, but much larger sums in side bets, which were eagerly reported by the newspapers. It is possible that some private race sponsors were in fact creating betting opportunities for themselves and their friends. Some wagers were frivolous, as in July 1793 when the yachts *Eclipse* and *Cumberland* sailed a wager match for a turtle, after which the owners and their friends dined on the prize. Other wagers were larger. The Earl of Wickham's yacht, the *Maria Ann*, raced the *Earl of Spencer* at Gravesend in 1800, and the *Sporting Magazine* commented: 'although the wager was only for 50 guineas, yet many thousands [guineas] changed masters'.[66] A consequence of heavy betting was that fouls and very rough tactics were almost the rule rather than the exception, and were frequently reported by the newspapers. For instance, in 1786 the yacht *Prince of Wales* was deliberately obstructed by other boats, 'but she got all clear by the use of handspikes', while the crew of the yacht *Don Giovanni* in 1824 found that 'they were towing twelve and a half fathoms of rope which was foul of either an old bolt or an old saucepan made fast to a spike gimlet bored into her stern'.[67]

The Formation of the Yacht Club at Cowes, 1815

English yachting acquired a new leader in 1815 when the Yacht Club was formally instituted to be based at London and Cowes. As noted earlier, the development of this club, later the Royal Yacht Squadron, was chronicled by Montague Guest and W.B. Boulton in 1903 and Ian Drear in 1985. Montague Guest, Librarian of the Royal Yacht Squadron, also compiled an invaluable series of scrapbooks of newspaper articles relating to yachting, which are preserved in the Squadron Library.

The formation of the Yacht Club in 1815 produced an undoubted social change in English organised yachting. The Thames yachtsmen, while wealthy enough to own pleasure boats, were rarely aristocrats, rather they were merchants, bankers, senior members of livery companies, lawyers and suchlike. For instance, William Hickey's Chelsea sailing and dining club included Mr James Bigger, of the East India Company, Alderman Kirkman, Mr Templer, later to be Master of the King's Bench, and Mr Adair, Recorder of London. The same social background characterised other Thames yachtsmen. In addition to Mr Smith of Smith's Tea Garden, Mr George Bellas, winner of the 1749 Prince of Wales Cup, was a registrar of Doctors' Commons, and Mr Condell, winner of the 1786 Jubilee Cup, was 'of the opera band'.[68] Thus sailing on the Thames it seems, had not been socially exclusive, possibly because the confined water available limited yacht size, so that most of the yachts raced on the Thames were under 10 tons.

However, in 1815 when the end of the Napoleonic War meant the Channel was free from privateers, a meeting in London led to the formal foundation by forty-two members of the socially exclusive club, Whites, of a yacht club, whose vessels were based at Cowes, on the Isle of Wight. Cowes was a port easily accessible from London, and handy to sheltered water in the Solent and Southampton Water. The subsequent progress of the Yacht Club was rapid. The Prince Regent and his brothers became members in 1817, and the society was granted a warrant as the Royal Yacht Club in 1820 when George IV became king. In 1833 it was designated the Royal Yacht Squadron, and became established as the social and practical centre of British yachting. The Yacht Club served several functions. Like other clubs it served its own members, provided conviviality among social equals, social sailing, and physical comfort. It was the first English sailing club, in 1825, to lease a club house, rather than meeting to dine at a tavern, coffee house, or tea garden.[69] It also had a profound influence on yachtsmen who would never be its own members.

The Yacht Club was from 1815 – and so it has remained – a centre of power, prestige, and hence privilege. The original forty-two members, with one exception, were aristocrats or landowners, including fourteen peers, or heirs to peers, and four baronets. A solitary City member, Sir William Curtis, noted as a cruising yachtsman and MP for the City for twenty-eight years, can probably be seen as an early example of the entry of the entrepreneur into such society.[70] The social rank of members remained high in succeeding years. In 1824 the ninety-six-member list included the king, two royal dukes, twelve peers, four baronets and four knights.[71] The elevated rank of the members of the Yacht Club ensured close personal contact and influence with government at the highest level, and this was used to obtain privileges for members. For instance, exemption from port dues paid by commercial ships in France, was obtained by the Marquis of Anglesea in 1820, using his personal contacts with his old Waterloo commander, the Duke of Wellington. Similar exemptions were later granted to the Club by most European governments. Personal contacts, particularly via Lord Yarborough and Lord Belfast, later secured and maintained Royal Yacht Squadron members' privileges, as members of a 'squadron' with semi-naval status, with regard to the use of Royal Navy dockyards for certain types of work, the right to use empty Navy moorings, treatment with the same courtesies as His Majesty's ships-of-war in foreign ports, and the right to wear the White Ensign, some of which privileges were later shared by other royal Yacht Clubs.[72]

The original regulations of the Yacht Club included a requirement that members should hold 'the ownership of a vessel not under 10 tons'. The list-size was raised to 20 tons in 1817, and 30 tons in 1825,[73] but most Yacht Club vessels were substantially larger than this, or any yachts then sailing on the Thames. For instance, in 1815 members owned thirty-five yachts, with an average size of 64 tons, and this had risen by 1824 to seventy-one yachts, with an average size of 67 tons.[74] These large yachts were obviously capable of long-distance cruising, and, since the club did not organise club racing for members before 1826, although wager matches took place, cruising was the principal mode of sailing used by members, supplemented by naval manoeuvres under the command of their commodore. The formation of the Yacht Club provided a body which, by virtue of its socially distinguished membership, was able to become the leading authority and source of influence in British yachting, had sufficient wealth among its members to influence yacht design, and whose presence was highly regarded at later provincial regattas as an economic asset.

It was previously noted that yacht cruising developed nationally, rather than in London alone, and racing under sail, although pioneered in London, also took place on rare occasions in other centres. For example, the Bristol Sailing Society held a race in 1796, while sailing races were held at Southampton in 1790, 1798 and 1802, and at Cowes in 1776, 1784 and 1788. Plate 2 shows an advertisement for a regatta held at Weymouth in 1782. Some owners went to considerable lengths to participate in regattas. The owner of the yacht *Peggy*, resident in the Isle of Man, had sufficient enthusiasm to sail his boat to the mainland, and then transport her by road from Penney Bridge, north of Ulverston, to Newby Bridge at the south end of

𝔚eymouth 𝔊rand 𝔕egatta

Or BOAT RACE,

For the *Honor* of the WESTERN COAST.

TO ALL OWNERS OF SWIFT SAILING

CUTTERS and LUGGERS,

Not exceeding *Twenty Tons* Burthen,

A PRIZE,

Of not lefs than TEN GUINEAS,

WILL be given to the Veffel that wins the Day, and alfo a handfome reward to the Second.

The Boats are to Start *from* and Come *in* at the *Pier head*, and to Sail round certain Boats, which will be ftationed for that purpofe.

There will alfo be a RACE of fmall failing Boats — and PRIZES given accordingly.

N. B. There will be a *Public Breakfaft*, and a *Band of Mufic* at the Great BALL ROOM at Ten in the Morning.

The whole to conclude with a *Ball* in the Evening, for the fupport and improvement of the *Public Walk*.

TICKETS 5s. each.

☞ As this FESTIVAL is held to celebrate and welcome the Arrival of the *ORESTES* Man of War, ftationed here by the Admiralty, for the Protection of the Trade and Coafts of this Neighbourhood. and Man'd folely by Brave and Spirited VOLUNTEERS Inhabitants of this Coaft and its Environs, We are affured, that no PRESS GANG will Moleft the honeft *Sailors* that attend the Feftival on that Day.

The *Regatta* will be held on *Wednefday*, the 4th of *September*.

✱.✱ SUBSCRIPTIONS from the *Nobility* and *Gentry* in the Neighbourhood will be received by the Mafter of the Ceremonies

Plate 2. Advertisement for Weymouth Grand Regatta, 1782. Source: C. B. Andrews, ed., *The Torrington Diaries: Containing the Tours through England and Wales of the Hon. John Byng (later 5th Viscount Torrington) between the years 1781 and 1794* (1934-6), 1,101.

Windermere to race in a regatta at Windermere in 1796.[75] The limited evidence of both widespread cruising and racing suggests that yachting and pleasure boat sailing was certainly not confined to London, but evolved quietly on most suitable water in and around Britain in the eighteenth and early nineteenth centuries. The development of cruising and racing in one such area, South Devon, will now be examined.

The Rise of Yachting in South Devon, 1700-1827

The first recorded yachting in South Devon took place in the early eighteenth century, and, since most rivers in the region are tidal and only navigable for a short distance from the mouth, developed, in spite of frequent wars, in the estuaries, on coastal waters, and in the Channel. The first regatta, or 'Fête Marine' was held in 1775. The concept, practice and organisation of yacht racing was probably imported from the Thames, and, as on the Thames, competitive sailing could only evolve once a substantial pleasure fleet had been established, and potential aristocratic patrons or commercial sponsors considered regattas, events which usually involved both competitive sailing and rowing, to be a profitable field for investment. No yacht clubs were formed in Devon before 1827, which probably reflects the fact that yachtsmen were more widely geographically dispersed than on the Thames.

Most Devon pleasure sailing craft were of interest only to their owner, builder, or potential purchasers, so that information regarding yachts in the county is relatively sparse for the years between 1700 and 1827. But various sources do exist from which the number, size, value, and modes of use of yachts owned and used in South Devon in this period can be estimated. These sources include: records of the use and sale of naval yachts; estate papers; newspaper advertisements for local yacht sales; newspaper reports of regattas and local maritime accidents; private journals and letters, both of local residents and visitors to the area; shipyard records, accounts and contracts; Custom House Shipping Registers for Exeter, Plymouth and Dartmouth (after 1786); and national yacht club records (after 1815).

The Number of Yachts in South Devon, 1700-1827

Royal Navy Yachts
The earliest yachts used in South Devon were Royal Navy vessels, five of which can be identified, from the *St Lo* (4 guns, 47 tons), built at Plymouth Dock in 1700, and sold when declared worn out in 1716,

to the *Plymouth* (6 guns, 96 tons), launched on 2 November 1796.[76] These Dockyard, or Admiralty, yachts were used for official business, the entertainment of distinguished visitors and private pleasure by the Commissioners of the Dockyard. In 1762 Sir Frederick Rogers, Commissioner, lent his yacht to take Dr Johnson out to see the Eddystone lighthouse.[77] The yacht was again noted in the newspaper in 1767, when the *Exeter Flying Post*, describing the visit of Princess Amelia to Plymouth, noted that, 'the colours on board the [Commissioner's] yacht all displayed at once, which made a delightful object', and reported that the yacht fired salutes.[78] The Admiralty yacht, 'decorated', was also noted as present at the Plymouth regatta of 1824.[79]

Estate Papers
Estate papers provide important sources from which yachts can be identified. The principal archives consulted for this period have included those of the Courtenays of Powderham Castle and Sir Francis Drake of Nutwell, both on the Exe estuary; the papers of Reginald Pole of Stoke Damerel, in the archives of Antony House, near Torpoint; and of Lord Boringdon, later the Earl of Morley, of Saltram House, Plymouth. Twenty yachts have been identified from estate papers for the period 1730-1827.

The Powderham Castle accounts and inventories show that the Courtenay family owned fourteen yachts and small pleasure boats between 1733 and 1811. Not all the yachts were described by name in the account books, but three bore the name *Dolphin* (from the dolphins in the Courtenay arms), and have, for the purposes of this study, been designated *Dolphin 1, 2 and 3*. Some building dates and sizes are uncertain, as some accounts are incomplete, and the vessels appeared in accounts or inventories when already in service. The list includes five major yachts, *Trew Blew*, *Neptune* and the three *Dolphins*.[80] The size and date of building of *Trew Blew* are not known. The first reference to a large yacht in the Powderham accounts is the payment in January 1736 of a crewman's wages which were eighteen months in arrears, so that a yacht was in service by August 1734. This was probably *Trew Blew*, since this vessel was used for major excursions until 1738, when *Dolphin 1* (80 tons) was built on the Thames.[81] The first *Dolphin* was advertised for sale in 1763,[82] and replaced by the *Neptune*, size unknown, built on the Exe by Worthington Brice of Lympstone. In 1787 the 70-ton yacht *Dolphin 2* was built for the second Lord Courtenay by John and James Wells at Deptford.[83] This yacht was still in good condition in 1811, as it was then used to take the third Lord Courtenay to residence in America, and presumed sold there, although no date of sale is known. *Dolphin 3*, a 163-ton brigantine, was added to the pleasure fleet in 1809, but repossessed and sold by the builder in 1811.[84]

In addition to the major yachts, the Courtenay family owned a number of smaller pleasure boats, presumably suitable for shorter coastal excursions worked by small crews. The *Bonetta* was inventoried in 1762, and the *Swallow* in 1789.[85] A 34-ton schooner yacht was advertised for sale by the estate in February 1802 as new. She did not find a purchaser, and was re-advertised in June 1803 and August 1804. Other boats included a 'new cutter', whose account was submitted by Worthington Brice in December 1768, and a 'small yacht' built in 1807 by Mr Owen of Topsham.[86] Repair bills were paid for 'pleasure boats' in 1733-6, but the small charges suggest craft which, like the small barge inventoried in 1762 and the lateen-rigged boat sold in 1811, were probably used for single-handed, family, or small party pleasure sailing in the shallow tidal waters of the Exe.[87] The evidence suggests that the Courtenay family between 1730 and 1811 maintained a range of pleasure boats, including large yachts suitable for Channel cruising, small sea-going yachts, which could be easily taken outside the Bar of the Exe for local cruises or fishing excursions, and very small craft for river use.

The Courtenay papers also identified yachts owned by other families, and thus suggested other avenues for research, as when a ledger detailed gratuities given by Sir William Courtenay to the crew of Sir Nicholas Trevannion's yacht in 1736; to 'the black on Mr Penlyres yatt', in the same year; and to Sir Francis Drake's crew in 1732 and 1733.[88] Sir Francis Drake of Buckland Abbey and Nutwell Court owned at least two yachts, since he entertained Sir William in 1732, and presumably purchased a second yacht before his death in 1743, as the summary of his debts at this time included payments of £80 to John Taylor for the yacht sloop, and £12.19s.4d. for ballast for the old *Nancy*.[89]

Yachts were built and maintained by other South Devon owners in the eighteenth century. Reginald Pole of Stoke Damerel, Plymouth, had a 'pleasure boat' built in 1745, and kept it for the next five years. It is most fortunate that a set of more than fifty bills for the construction, fitting out and maintenance of this yacht survive. The bills do not state the size of the boat, but the anchor and sail size suggest 10-20 tons. The vessel carried two guns, and hammocks, so was presumably capable of sea-going passages of some length.[90] In contrast young Lord Boringdon, later the Earl of Morley, at Saltram House, by the very shallow tidal Laira River, bought a modest pleasure boat in 1795. The yacht was used by his sister in 1796 when he was absent from home, and the excursion was described in a letter to her aunt: 'I have just been sailing about on the Lairy for two hours ... there is a very safe boat here now that my brother bought this year past'.[91]

Newspapers

From the mid-eighteenth century, newspapers, both local and national, provide valuable information on South Devon yachts by the publication of advertisements of vessels for sale and hire, reports of marine accidents, and reports of regattas and other yachting activities.

Sixty-seven South Devon yachts, or vessels which may have been used for pleasure-sailing, have been identified from newspaper advertisements. It is not easy to identify yachts with certainty among vessels advertised for sale in the eighteenth century, since many craft advertised as yachts had not been built for that purpose, and were advertised as suitable for a variety of uses. In 1806 the cutter *Diana* (102 tons) was advertised as, 'well calculated for His Majesty's Custom or Excise service, a privateer, yacht, [or] packet'.[92] Also, the naval prize *Impromtu*, taken in 1799, was offered as suitable for 'Pacquet, Guineaman, Yacht or any other purpose'.[93] Similarly, some yachts were advertised as equally suitable for other purposes. Lord Courtenay's aristocratic brigantine, *Dolphin 3*, sold in 1811, was advertised as 'a nobleman's yacht ... would make a desirable vessel for the fruit trade'.[94] Some yachts were promoted as privateers, such as the *Dart*, advertised in 1789 as, 'frigate built, 235 tons, 14 guns ... built and furnished purposely for a gentleman's yacht ... would make an excellent sloop of war'.[95] Other vessels were advertised as yachts or fishing boats. The *Sylph,* in 1795, was 'fitted up as a yacht and trawl boat, for either of which purposes she is extremely well adapted'.[96]

By the early nineteenth century many newspaper advertisements stressed the speed and/or elegant accommodation of purpose-built yachts. In 1812 purchasers were offered a yacht which 'contains an elegantly fitted up cabin, bed places, a dining room, watercloset and gallery'.[97] The owner of the *Charlotte* in 1811 stressed her racing record: 'Sails ... well, having won the cup at Teignmouth this summer'.[98] At the other end of the market small pleasure boats were advertised, such as a 22-foot pleasure boat, complete with masts and sails, at Exmouth in 1813.[99] Yachtsmen could also charter. The yacht *Eleanor* was advertised in 1771 as available for private charter at two hours notice.[100] Table 2 shows the yachts identified by newspaper advertisements in South Devon between 1754 and 1827.

Table 2
Yachts Advertised for Sale in South Devon Newspapers, 1754-1827

	Multi-purpose vessels, suggested possible use as yacht	Vessel built as a yacht, or converted to a yacht, and in use as such before sale	Total
1751-60	1	-	1
1761-70	1	4	5
1771-80	1	2	3
1781-90	2	4	6
1791-1800	2	5	7
1801-10	7	15	22
1811-20	6	10	16
1821-27	2	5	7
Totals	22	45	67

Sources: *Exeter Flying Post*; *Sherborne and Yeovil Mercury*; *Plymouth and Dock Gazette*; *Plymouth Weekly*; *Plymouth Herald*; for the period 1754-1827.

It will be seen that yacht advertisements were sparse until the decade 1801-10, when there was a sudden surge of notices. As will be seen later, this was the period which saw the start of regular regatta activity. A high advertisement level was maintained for the next decade, then dropped away somewhat. This decrease probably does not indicate any lack of interest in the years 1821-7, since other sources show an increase of yachting activity during these years, but is more likely to reflect the growing practice of transfer of vessels through yacht agents.

Table 2 includes only those vessels identified as yachts, or sold with an advertised possible use as yachts, and as such can only give an approximate estimate of advertised vessels which later sailed as yachts in local waters. Some vessels advertised as yachts may have been used for other purposes after sale, or may have been sold out of the area. Other pleasure craft may have been bought in from the South Coast or Cornwall, after response to advertisements in national newspapers, or in local newspapers serving other areas. It should also be noted that the boats advertised as yachts do not represent the complete spectrum of vessels available in the years considered above. The South Devon newspapers also contained many advertisements for small sloops, cutters and schooners sold as new vessels, as privateer prizes, and after Customs seizure, which could easily be converted to pleasure use. An example of this type of advertisement is one in 1797 for 'the good lugger *Swallow*, a most admirable fast sailer, 62 tons, built at Plymouth not three years since ... lately taken on a contraband trade on her passage from France by H.M.S. *Lively*'.[101] There were, of course, other smaller vessels used for pleasure sailing which do not figure in sale advertisements, but, then as now, were sold by personal contact and word of mouth within the ports.

South Devon yachts, and other boats used occasionally for pleasure, can also be identified from accidents or crimes reported in newspapers. Reports on accidents in South Devon between 1733-1827 identified twenty pleasure boats, and indicated a wide social range among those who sailed for pleasure, since the persons reported as involved in Devon pleasure-boat accidents included more than seven gentlemen (one report mentions 'several gentlemen'), two clergymen, four ladies, sixteen men (one a servant), eighteen women (three of these servants), and three children (one an apprentice). Twenty-six deaths were reported. As many women as men were involved in sailing accidents, although at this period, like many of the men, they were probably passengers, rather than taking an active part in the sailing.[102]

Yachting accidents arose from shipwreck, capsize, or transfer between yachts and tenders. For instance, Lieutenant Hamilton Clarke and his wife, another gentleman and two boatmen capsized their dinghy when boarding a yacht in 1779 at Exmouth, drowning the lady and one of the boatmen.[103] At Plymouth in 1814, Lieutenant Hooper of Torpoint was 'amusing himself with his pleasure boat in Hamoaze', crewed by his father's 16-year old apprentice, when the boat capsized in a squall and the youth was drowned.[104] Also, the yacht *Agile* of Torquay, on passage to Brixham in March 1815, was lost off Berry Head, drowning a youth, described as 'a young man bred to the sea, a zealous preacher ... intended for a foreign mission', and the boatman, 'an excellent young man whose services were devoted to a strict and upright discharge of the duties of that station in life, in which it has pleased God to place him'. A young woman in the boat also lost her life. Four years later Reverend Bellfield was more fortunate when he ran the *Gleaner* on to the rocks at Babbacombe and all his crew survived.[105] There were several cases reported of yachts capsizing in the Exe. In 1815, for instance, a party of 'one man and three women, all servants, pleasuring in a boat in the Bight at Exmouth', capsized by running across the hawser of a collier.[106] Possibly the most tragic accident in this period was the loss, in 1815, of ten young people from Otterton, when a sailing boat taking a party of fifteen on an excursion following a wedding ceremony capsized, drowning nine young women, including the bride and her sister, and one man.[107] Yachts and yachting activity can also be identified by such reports as that of the death, probably from a heart attack, of a retired Newfoundland Captain, who attempted to secure a small yacht in his care at Exmouth in an October gale in 1794. There was also the theft and subsequent wreck of a yacht at Exmouth by escaping French prisoners of war in 1800; and the experiences of two Teignmouth gentlemen who visited Cherbourg in August 1814, subsequently went into the town for a meal 'where they met with much incivility', and returned to the harbour to find their yacht vandalized.[108]

Newspapers, local and national, also provide information on local yachts and their users in the form of regatta reports. The reported race entries between 1775 and 1827, for instance, included 395 yachts,[109] but several factors indicate that this must be regarded as a minimum figure. Contemporary newspapers did not record all advertised regattas, particularly if the limited news-space available was under pressure from other items. For example, yacht races and regattas were advertised, but not reported, at Starcross in 1799 and 1801, at Teignmouth in 1807, 1808, 1812 and 1813, and at Torquay in 1811, 1813 and 1814. Some interesting information was provided by an advance review of the Teignmouth regatta of 1808, which stated that ten gentlemen's yachts had entered.[110] Published reports often gave very limited information on the yachts present. The *Exeter Flying Post* report of the Exmouth Regatta of 1821, for instance, noted only the social aspects of the event, which 'was attended by a very genteel and numerous company. The prizes were well contested, about 150 fashionables partook of the public breakfast and the Ball in the evening ... was well attended. Rural sports amused the populace after the boat races'. No yachts were mentioned. Also some regatta reports mentioned only the winning or placed yachts, as in the report of the 1816 Teignmouth event, when the public breakfast, the 'cold collation' served at 3 pm, and the Ball were described in detail, and the name of the winner of the first-class race was given as an afterthought.[111] However, in spite of these limitations, the figure of 395 reported regatta entries between 1775 and 1827, while it has to be seen as a minimum figure, shows that yachting was a robust sport in this period in South Devon.

Journals Kept by Visitors to South Devon

A further minor source for the identification of South Devon yachts in the second half of the eighteenth century is provided by the journals of visitors to the county. From these accounts six yachts have been identified. Fanny Burney in 1773, for instance, described an excursion in a yacht owned by the Reverend Hurrell of Tedburn St Mary, from Teignmouth to see the Fleet in Torbay. The vessel, in company with another yacht, was driven by bad weather into Brixham overnight.[112] Other travellers had more enjoyable experiences. For instance, in 1797 William Maton hired a yacht to go up the Tamar to visit the lead mines at Bere Alston,[113] while Mrs Lybbe Powys in 1760 hired a sailing boat, visited Mount Edgcumbe, saw the fortifications on Drake's Island, and was 'wafted to the Dock'.[114] William Gilpin, who in 1799 borrowed a boat and crew from H.M.S. *Ocean* to sail up the Tamar, landed at Cotehele and noted 'here we refreshed ourselves with tea and larded our bread, after the fashion of the country, with clouted cream'.[115] Some visitors' journals and newspaper reports of public events suggest that South Devon had a large pleasure fleet of small sailing boats. George Lipscomb, in 1794, sailing up the Tamar to Saltash and Trematon, commented on 'the busy assemblage of aquatic adventurers who had been drawn together by the fineness of the weather',[116] while when, in 1789, George III visited Plymouth, the *Exeter Flying Post* reported that 'their Majesties, in rowing up Catwater, received salutes and huzzas from upwards of 200 yatchs and pleasure boats'.[117]

The Customs House Registers

More reliable evidence on the larger yachts based in South Devon becomes available from 1786 when the Merchant Shipping Act of that year established a legal requirement for decked vessels of over 15 tons to register. The Registers do not supply a complete record of yachts in South Devon, as the smaller boats are not included. Moreover, the records are not complete, since the Dartmouth and Plymouth transcripts from 1786 to 1814 were lost in the London Custom House fire of 1814.[118] However, the Exeter Registers are available from 1786, and the Plymouth and Dartmouth Registers from 1814, so that some earlier vessels can be identified by extrapolation from post-1814 entries. The Custom House Shipping Registers provide details of vessel size, rig, builder, date and place of construction, ownership, and changes of ownership. Yachts were not named as such, although some registrars' notes did identify them, but they can be identified by vessel size, rig, and by the status of the owner or series of owners.

Table 3 shows the yachts registered in South Devon between 1786 and 1827.

Table 3
The Number and Rig of Yachts Registered in South Devon, 1786-1827

	Schooner	Cutter	Sloop	Other Rig	Total	Sold
1786-1799						
Exeter	1	2	4	-	7	4
1801-15						
Dartmouth	-	2	1	-	--	-
Exeter	-	-	4	2	13	2
Plymouth	1	1	1	1	-	-
1816-20						
Dartmouth	-	1	-	1	-	-
Exeter	-	1	-	1	8	5
Plymouth	-	1	1	2	-	-
1821-7						
Dartmouth	1	3	-	-	-	-
Exeter	1	1	-	-	13	7
Plymouth	1	4	-	2	-	-
Totals	5	16	11	9	41	18

Sources: DRO, Custom House Shipping Registers, Exeter, 1786-1827; PRO, Plymouth and Dartmouth Registers, 1814-24; DRO, Dartmouth Registers, 1824-7; WDRO, Plymouth Registers, 1824-7.

As the table shows, a minimum of forty-one yachts were registered in the registry ports of Exeter, Dartmouth and Plymouth between 1786 and 1827, with the cutter most popular. Several yachts used local rigs, including a smack-rigged vessel, a lugger, and several vessels were described as 'pleasure boats', normally half-decked and with a cuddy, but rig unspecified. Twenty-seven of the yachts registered were Devon-built, and most of the owners described themselves as 'gentleman', or 'esquire'. Yachts were also registered by a peer, a barrister, an attorney, five naval officers and an architect. The table also shows that yachts did not always stay in the area after registration, eighteen yachts being sold out of South Devon during the period.

Yacht Club Records and Membership Lists
There were no Devon yacht clubs set up in the period before 1827, but six South Devon yachts are identifiable from the records of the Royal Yacht Squadron.[119]

Shipyard Accounts, Contracts, and Yacht Agents' Letters
Finally, for the early nineteenth century, yachts can be identified by boatyard accounts and contracts, auctioneers' documents, and yacht agents' letters to prospective customers. Three additional yachts have been identified from these sources.

Total of the Larger Yachts Used in South Devon, 1730-1827
Table 4 summarises the information on the larger yachts in South Devon that can be obtained from the sources just discussed. Care has been taken to avoid, as far as possible, any double counting, so that some figures given in the table differ from those quoted above. It should also be noted that the yachts have been allocated to the two groups shown in the table on the basis of the first date on which they were recorded, so that many of those in the group 1730-1815, would still have been active after 1816.

Table 4
The Number of Larger Yachts in South Devon, 1730-1827

	1730-1815	1816-27
Navy records	5	-
Estate records	20	-
Newspaper advertisements	58	9
Reported accidents	15	5
Regatta entries	84+	292+
Visitors' journals	6	-
Customs House registers	20	21
Royal Yacht Squadron	-	4
Shipyard records	1	2
Totals	209	333

Sources: As for Table 3 above.

As has been stated, these figures of 209 known yachts between 1730 and 1815, and 333 between 1816 and 1827, are almost certainly underestimates. The data does, however, show that pleasure sailing was well established in South Devon waters before the end of the French wars in 1815, and the surge of the newspaper advertisements of yachts in the years 1801-10, as shown in Table 2, underlines the fact that privateer activity in the Channel did not deter the expansion of yachting. The large numerical difference shown in Table 4 between the yachts present in the area and the yachts registered in the area also suggests that the majority of South Devon owners, then as now, used craft of less than 15 tons which did not need registration. This is supported by the fact that most early regattas in the area offered races for small yachts, as at Torquay in 1822, when, in addition to a race for yachts under 50 tons, a second race was for 'gentlemen's decked or open yachts under 15 tons', and a third for 'gentlemens' decked or open boats under 21 feet aloft, stem to stern'.[120] It is not difficult to accept (allowing for some press exaggeration) the previously noted figure of 'upwards of 200 yatchs and pleasure boats' said to have greeted George III at Plymouth in 1789.[121]

The Costs of South Devon Yachting, 1730-1827

Some information is available on the cost as well as the numbers of South Devon yachts in this period. Yacht owners faced capital costs, in the purchase and equipping of vessels, and maintenance charges. We are fortunate to have some surviving yacht accounts, principally those of the Courtenay family, but also from Reginald Pole of Stoke Damerel.

The Courtenay yachts, as has been noted, covered a wide range of size, and hence of value, from the £52 paid for a small cutter in 1768 to £3,900 for the brigantine *Dolphin 3* in 1809.[122] The Courtenays, like other owners, found that the final cost of a new yacht was often considerably more than the basic charge agreed with the builder. For instance, when the *Dolphin 1* was built in 1738 on the Thames, the basic charge was £420 for hull and masts. In addition £63.10s. was spent on sails, and additional charges were made for ballast, chandlery and a small boat. These, with charges for upholstery and other interior fitting-out expenses, raised the cost to £777.17s.8d. before the yacht left the shipyard. Sir William paid the traditional tips to workmen at the launch and completion, coupled with extra gratuities 'for hurraying the yacht'. Although the owner maintained a London house for his own use, he paid the expenses of the crew of *Trew Blew*, who had come to London to take the new yacht home, as well as the coach and watermen's charges for his frequent trips to the yard to observe the building process. Finally, the voyage home for the two yachts, with the expenses of extra crewmen hired for the passage, accounted for more than £50. While the basic cost of the hull was £420, the total amount paid out before the vessel was in use on the Exe was nearly £900.[123] A similar situation arose with *Dolphin 2*, built at Deptford. The boat-yard account submitted in June 1787 detailed a cost of £770. However, a 'memorandum' in another hand was written on the bill, noting that the total cost included £103.12s.3d. for cordage, £67.3s.4d. for sails, £19 for blocks and £735 for 'London Bills', making a total of £1,695.3s.9d.[124]

The cost of yacht maintenance at Powderham Castle has been difficult to estimate from the entries in the account books. Some items though were clearly expenditure on individual yachts. For instance, in 1763: 'To Betty Cruise for mending the colours belonging to the *Bonetta* yacht, 2 shillings.'[125] Others were mingled with other estate expenditure, as with, 'Nov. 30 1769, paid Mr George Jackson of Topsham, a bill of cordage for the yachts and rope yarn for the thatchers, £12.3s.6½d.'[126] However, yacht expenditure, at least in 1809, can be seen in the context of general estate expenditure, as the steward then reviewed Lord Courtenay's expenditure, with suggestions for retrenchment. A summary of this document is given in Table 5.

Table 5
Viscount Courtenay's Expenditure in 1809, with his Steward's
Suggestions for Retrenchment

	1809 Expenditure £	Suggestions for Revised Expenditure £
Servants' wages (noted as 'low')	909	909
Board wages and household bills	4290	3000
Grocery from London	900	500
Wine and spirits	960	600
Malt	200	360
Coal and charcoal	840	840
Coachmakers, saddlers, keep of horses	2000	846
Tailor, hatter, shoemaker, stocking bill	2962	1200
YACHT [author's capitals]	600	600
Upholsterer, London, Exeter and on yacht	5000	100

House rent London	300	300
Silversmith, glass and china	500	150
Estate improvements, repairs, alterations	2020	600
Painter, plasterer, smith, cooper, brazier	2720	750
Wheelwright, glazier, mason, carpenter	810	450
Labourers wages, farm and garden	1300	1300
Taxes, town and country	1000	1000
Viscount Courtenay's private purse	3000	3000
	£30311	£16505
	Reduced by	13806
		£30311

Source: DRO, 1508M, Statement prepared by the steward for Lord Courtenay, 1809.

Table 5 shows that the yacht (presumably a blanket term covering all the pleasure boats), while a significant item in estate expenditure, was not one of the major expenses. £600 was considered a reasonable maintenance sum, or an item where reduction would be unacceptable to Lord Courtenay, since it appeared unchanged in the revised budget. No indication was given of the 'yacht' share of the massive £5000 spent on upholstery in 1809. Yacht expenditure was only a half of the suggested tailors', shoemakers', and hatters' bills in the revised budget, and was equal to the money to be spent on wine. The yacht annual maintenance was some two per cent of the actual budget for 1809, and 3.6 per cent of the reformed budget suggested for 1810.

It was possible for a gentleman to build and maintain a yacht at much lower cost. Mr Reginald Pole, of Stoke Damerel near Plymouth, kept a pleasure boat, for which the building and upkeep bills survive for the period 1745-52. The yacht cost £127.9s.5d. to build, including sails, a mainsail of 90 square yards, 'graet geeb, 42 yd of Rucchia duck', 'small geeb 26½ yards', 'foresaile 38yd' and guns. Maintenance charges were also light, a total of £2.17s.9½d. in 1747, £13.2s.8d. in 1748, £23.15s.10d. in 1749, and £2.1s.4½d. in 1750. Maintenance charges were light for the first year after building was completed, but a new mast and top-gallant yard were needed in 1748, and a major refit took place in 1749. Painting was a complex operation, since it involved the preparation of paint from white and red lead, with other

135

chemicals to give the colours required, in addition to rubbing-down and the application of the paint. In 1749 the yacht was painted in red, yellow, white and black, with some bright work, and included a labour charge of £1.11s., not unreasonable when the painter was working for fifteen and a half days. The 1750 painting was simpler, the painter charging only for 'four days grinding and painting'.[127]

Other information on yacht prices is sparse for the period. It is not easy to obtain figures for the prices of yachts and small pleasure boats sold or offered for sale in South Devon in the period, since most vessels were sold by auction, by the candle, or by private contract, and such price records are rare, but some builders' contracts and yacht agents' letters dealing with large yachts survive. For example, the nearby Cornish yard of Henna and Dunn at Mevagissey built the 14-ton *Sir Sydney Smith* in 1809 for £266, and the Royal Yacht Club vessel *Eliza* (41 tons), belonging to the Dartmouth resident Stephen Challen, was on the market in 1823 at £700. George Hooke of Exmouth contracted to build a 22-ton yacht for £154 in 1826, while the *Transit* (34 tons) was sold (second-hand) in 1826 for £300.[128]

Mode of Use of South Devon Yachts, 1730-1827

The major modes of yacht use, and the only ones available in South Devon before 1775, were day-sailing and cruising, both long and short-distance, and recreational fishing. Local yachts were augmented in the season by visiting vessels who exchanged courtesies with local gentry. For instance, Lord Uxbridge in 1783 arrived in Plymouth on a cruise, was sent a gift of venison by Lord Borringdon, then called at Saltram House and invited the ladies of the household to a water party on board his yacht.[129] Local owners also made off-shore cruises, as when Lord Courtenay, as noted earlier, visited Guernsey in 1790, obviously in rough conditions, as a boom was replaced on the island, and a new mast was fitted by Moore of Plymouth on the way home. As with modern yachtsmen visiting the Channel Isles, the opportunity was taken to bring back alcoholic refreshment, and Lord Courtenay brought back claret and other wine, on which he paid £40.2s.9½d. at the Custom House, then sold twenty dozen of the claret to Lord Charles Somerset, 'the prime cost being £30 and the duty £10.16s.6d.'. Lord Courtenay was at Southampton in *Dolphin 3* in July 1810.[130]

Most local voyages, it appears, were shorter, with country gentleman using their yachts for local transport, as well as pleasure mixed with business. Sir William Courtenay visited Plymouth on business in *Trew Blew* in 1836, but paid a social visit *en route* to Sharpham on the Dart, and was later entertained on Mr Penlyre's 'yatt', where he tipped the crew. At Plymouth Sir William arranged a sale of timber to the Dockyard, the contract for which was drawn up on Sir Nicholas Trevannion's yacht.[131] This was presumably the Admiralty yacht *Drake*, as Sir Nicholas was the Commissioner of the Dockyard between 1726-37.[132] Sir William bought 'a galloon of sherry for the yatchs', and half a barrel of gunpowder at Plymouth and returned via his estates at Salcombe. The cost of the excursion was £36.3s.9½d. In 1737 Sir William took his wife for a cruise in the yacht to Dartmouth and Salcombe.[133] The Courtenay yacht *Neptune* went to London for sale in 1788.[134] There are sparse records of the cruising activity of other South Devon owners, but Stephen Challen was in the Solent with the *Eliza* in 1821, as he acted as Royal Yacht Club Commodore in manoeuvres in Stokes Bay.[135]

Other local yacht excursions made by smaller boats can be identified from accident reports. In 1786, for instance, 'some gentlemen of Topsham, going out for a few days on a pleasure party' sprang a leak off the Exe Bar and were rescued by a fishing boat, while in another case two officers paid-off from a frigate at Plymouth in 1815, who had bought a small sailing boat to take themselves and their luggage to Deal, capsized while still in the Tamar, with the loss of all the luggage. Also the two yachts, the *Amazon* and the *Lady of the Lake*, were on passage from Plymouth to Exmouth in 1820, when they were caught in a gale, and against expectations, survived the approach to Exmouth harbour, watched by most of the townsfolk. The crew of the *Lady of the Lake* included Mr Reed and Lieutenant Reed, the latter being rebuked by the newspaper for taking his 'aged parent' on the expedition.[136]

Many gentlemen's yachts were used for serious recreational fishing, even the most elaborate Courtenay vessels. The Powderham yacht inventories do not include trawls, but the *Dolphin 1* carried a harpoon, fishgig and shark hook, and *Dolphin 3* in 1809 had 4 whiting lines and 4 'mackrell' lines,[137] while the Courtenay 'master of the yachts', John Hackworthy, supplemented his income by the supply of fish, crabs and lobsters to the castle kitchen, fishing even when his employer was on board. This is shown by an account book entry in 1798 of a payment 'to John Hackworthy for fish brought over the Bar when out with my Lord, 4s.6d'.[138]

Trawling was common from yachts in the eighteenth and early nineteenth centuries. In 1746 Reginald Pole had a trawl, made by Mary Put of Brixham, on his pleasure boat,[139] and in 1789 a 14-ton yacht, 'in good repair, with small boat, trawl, etc.', was sold at Exmouth.[140] Trawling was not restricted to cheap vessels. For instance, a pleasure yacht was advertised at Seaton in 1808 as equipped with 'everything that belongs to her, a trawl and trawl gear, two brass cannons and twelve tons of iron ballast'. The yacht was re-advertised eight months later as 'elegantly furnished', still with her trawl, and a note that she had been sold for £600 on the previous advertisement.[141] In 1811 the yacht *Swift*, property of the late George Box Esq., was advertised complete with sails, anchor and hawser, mooring, ensign, pendant, two sweeps, one trawl and beam and four small swivels.[142]

The Development of Yacht Racing and Regattas in South Devon

We turn now to the more competitive and commercially exploited aspects of South Devon yachting. Boat racing was not a traditional local sport. Although we can be sure that sailors have always raced each other on an informal basis, both for pleasure and, in the case of pilot boats, for commercial advantage, no evidence has been found of an organised sport of racing under sail or oars in South Devon before the end of the eighteenth century.

The first clear case of boat racing for pleasure occurred on the Exe in 1775, when a parade of sail and a rowing race took place at Starcross, officially hosted by the Starcross Club, a dining club of local gentlemen, a leading member of whom was Lord Courtenay. The event took place one month after a major rowing regatta, the first event to be so named in England, had taken place on the Thames. The Starcross event was a spectacular, successful, and locally sensational episode of aristocratic display, which involved not only a rowing race and a parade of sail by twenty sailing boats, on the pattern of the Cork Water Club and the Cumberland Fleet, but also illuminations, fireworks and a Ball. The 'Fête Marine' attracted huge crowds, and, according to the *Exeter Flying Post*, work in the county stopped for the day.[143]

A 'regatta' took place at Starcross, sponsored by Lord Courtenay, in 1786.[144] The death of the second Viscount Courtenay in 1788 and the majority of the third viscount in 1789 seems to have unleashed a spectacular period of conspicuous consumption at Powderham, one aspect of which was a series of sailing races at Starcross. In 1799 Lord Courtenay presented prizes for a sailing race on the Exe, and similar annual contests followed until 1802. These events clearly provided their sponsor with the opportunity for personal display. For instance, in 1800: 'His Lordship embarked on board his elegant barge ... accompanied by another barge having a band of music on board. A cannon was immediately fired, the band struck up "God Save the King" and the boats got under weigh.' In 1802, 'the elegant yachts of his lordship were dressed in their colours'.

Between 1799 and 1802 the races attracted large crowds, as in 1802 when there was, 'a very large assemblage of company, in carriages, on horses, and pedestrians', who lined the shore.[145] The Courtenay sailing parades and races were popular with yachtsmen and other boat-owners, as well as with spectators. The parade at the Fête Marine in 1775 included Lord Courtenay's yachts, the *Bee* yacht, and the 'Exmouth yacht, accompanied by a band of music ... and several members of the Society'. There were also 'several other vessels and boats from Topsham, Lympstone and the neighbourhood, about 20 in number and full of Company'. Twenty-two sailing boats raced at Starcross in 1800 and fifteen in 1802, and yachts came from Plymouth for these races, since the first prize in 1800 was won by Mr Thompson's boat of Plymouth, and the silver cup in 1802 by 'a gentleman of Stonehouse'.[146]

As in London, aristocratic patronage was followed by commercial sponsorship. The promoters of the rising health and holiday resorts, at Teignmouth and Exmouth (the nearest towns to Starcross), and later Torquay, had doubtless noted the popularity of the Starcross sailing races, particularly as Sir Robert Palk, Lord of the Manor of Torquay, and his heir, later Sir Lawrence Palk, prime developer of the town, were in 1775 members of the Starcross Club.[147] It is not easy to identify the time at which 'Boat Races', became 'regattas', as the word 'regatta' in late eighteenth-century England could be used for a race, under sail or oars, or an event. For instance, an American visitor in 1789 noted in his journal that he had watched a 'regatta or boat-race [rowing]' at Starcross, and as late as 1824 an English visitor to South Devon, Lady Sylvester, used the word in both senses in her journal. Recording a visit to Teignmouth Regatta, she noted that 'at all the regattas disputes arose about the winning vessel'.[148] Some events advertised as 'boat races', concluded with balls, as in the case of the Torquay 'Boat Race' of 1811.[149] However, during the early nineteenth century, the South Devon resorts adopted, developed and exploited the concept of the 'regatta' as an all-day social event with some maritime episodes, as a means to attract visitors, preferably upper-class, to the town. South Devon regattas offered races for rowing boats, and, depending on the value of the prizes which the sponsors were willing and able to provide, races for yachts and sailing boats of all sizes, from those over 50 tons to, as at Exmouth in 1819, boats under 16 feet in length.[150] Regattas were financed by a combination of subscriptions from townsmen, tradesmen and landowners who stood to gain from town development, race entry fees and charges made for public breakfasts and balls.

The South Devon regattas expanded after 1821. The Royal Yacht Club at Cowes had no club races between 1815 and 1825, but used their yachts in cruising, naval manoeuvres, and private wager matches.[151] The South Devon resorts, from 1821, attempted to exploit this situation by the provision of races for large yachts, with appropriate prizes, hoping to attract the Cowes yachts, and to provide an extra spectacle for the entertainment of holiday visitors. Reports of South Devon regattas between 1821 and 1827 show that two Royal Yacht Club boats raced in 1821, five in 1822, four in 1823, nine in 1824, six in 1825, five in 1826 and eleven in 1817.[152] These numbers were small, but the Cowes yachts normally cruised westwards in company, and the South Devon regattas provided other, non-racing members of the Royal Yacht Club and their families and guests, with opportunities to cruise in company, and attend regattas which provided spectator sport and opportunities for betting, display, and social contact. From the point of view of the regatta sponsors the presence of these spectacular vessels alone was enough to attract spectators. For instance, in 1824, although only three of the Cowes yachts raced at the Torquay Regatta, thirty club yachts were present, and it was reported that '20,000 persons lined the hills around'.[153] Further, in 1826 the steamer *Sir Francis Drake*, was able to take 'several loads of passengers' to view the races at the Plymouth Regatta at close quarters, with the bonus that 'for the greater gratification of her company she steered close to the beautiful and warlike yacht of Lord Yarborough, the Commodore of the Royal Yacht Club'.[154] It was unfortunate for Teignmouth that one result of increased participation by the large Royal Yacht Club vessels was that the focus of yacht racing moved from Teignmouth to the deeper water and safer anchorages of Torquay, Dartmouth and Plymouth.

Conclusion

It can thus be seen that the conventional version of English yachting history needs to be viewed with some caution. The use of pleasure boats under sail, and the word 'yacht' were not introduced into England by Charles II in 1660. The word 'yacht' was in practical use at least seventeen years previously at Herstmonceaux, and Charles II himself used a pleasure boat before his Dutch exile. The king probably developed a long-standing interest in Holland, and when he returned in 1660 had the financial resources to pursue his hobby, which was linked to naval development and the social influence to popularise it among the Court. A limited national interest in yachts and cruising survived the Stuart monarchy and developed through the eighteenth century in coastal and inland waters. Yachting developed as a popular spectator sport upon the Thames in the eighteenth and early nineteenth century, combining club formation (a social characteristic of Londoners) and yacht racing, both made possible by the presence of a large population, with sections sufficiently wealthy for yacht ownership, aristocratic and royal sponsors, and commercial sponsors, who could see potential profit from the large crowds drawn by yacht races. In 1815 the formation of the Yacht Club provided a wealthy and highly influential group of yachtsmen based on the South Coast at Cowes. It would, however, be an error to suppose that yachting was confined to the Thames because of coastal dangers from privateers in this period. It has been shown that racing took place outside the Thames from 1790, in regions as far apart as Bristol, the Lake District and Cowes, while cruising took place in coastal waters and further afield.

A more particular study of South Devon yachting shows that local residents owned yachts, used for cruising, business and fishing, at least from 1733, that there was a brisk seventeenth- and early eighteenth-century local market in second-hand yachts and pleasure boats, and a significant number of regatta entries, so that minimum figures of 209 yachts can be identified in the region between 1730 and 1815, and 333 between 1816 and 1827. There was also a significant amount of smaller yacht or sailing boat activity in these decades. The first organised yachting event was held in the area in 1775, probably in imitation of the regatta held the same year on the Thames, and this was followed by a series of yacht races sponsored by Lord Courtenay of Powderham. When the period of aristocratic sponsorship ended, however, as on the Thames, regattas were sponsored by commercial interests, in the case of South Devon by the developing holiday resorts. It is worth noting that far from a culture of yachting being diffused from the Royal Yacht Club at Cowes after 1815, the regattas in South Devon were established well before the Royal Yacht Club started to race in 1826, and that, between 1821 and 1825, South Devon was in a position to offer competition that was not available at Cowes.

NOTES

List of abbreviations

CRO	Cornish Record Office, Truro
DRO	Devon Record Office, Exeter
DoRO	Dorset Record Office, Dorchester
ERO	Essex Record Office, Chelmsford
NLS	National Library of Scotland, Edinburgh
PCA	Powderham Castle Archives
PRO	Public Record Office
RTYC	Royal Thames Yacht Club Records
RYS	Royal Yacht Squadron Library, Cowes
WDRO	West Devon Record Office, Plymouth

Unless otherwise stated all books are assumed to be published in London.

1   Thorstein Veblen, *The Theory of the Leisure Class: An Economic Study of Institutions* (New York, 1931 edn.).
2   Arthur H. Clark, *The History of Yachting, 1600-1815* (New York Yacht Club and London, 1904); compiled by *The Yachtsman, British Yachts and Yachtsmen: A Complete History of Yachting from the Middle of the Seventeenth Century to the Present Day* (1907); Douglas Phillips-Birt, *The Cumberland Fleet: Two Hundred Years of Yachting, 1775-1975* (1978); Montague Guest and W.B. Boulton, *The Royal Yacht Squadron: Memorials of its Members* (Cowes, 1903); Ian Drear, *The Royal Yacht Squadron, 1815-1985* (1985); G.H. Brierley and H.J. Grandison, *Souvenir of Torbay Royal Regattas: 1813-1913* (Torquay, 1913); S.F. Thomas, *Early History of the Teignmouth Regatta* (Teignmouth, 1995).
3   Giulia Bolgna, *Illuminated Manuscripts: The Book before Gutenberg* (1988), 159.
4   Richard Ferris, 'The most dangerous and memorable adventure of Richard Ferris ...' (1590), in J. Payne Collier, *Illustrations of Early English Popular Literature* (1863, New York, 1966 edn), II, 3-15.
5   William Falconer, *A Universal Dictionary of the Marine* (1780, David and Charles reprint, Newton Abbot, 1970), 327.
6   *The Oxford English Dictionary* (Oxford, 1935 edn), XII, 12.
7   Sir William Lower, *A Relation of the Voyage and Residence which His Most Excellent Majesty Charles II, King of Great Britain etc. has made in Holland from 25th May to 2 of June 1660* (1660), 26.

8   William Bray, ed., *The Diary of John Evelyn F.R.S.* (1818), 339.

9   *The Oxford English Dictionary* (Oxford, 1935 edn), XII, 12.

10   T. Barrett Lennard, 'Extracts from the household account book of Herstmonceaux Castle: from August 1643 to December 1649', *Sussex Archaeological Collections, XLVIII* (1905), 104-37.

11   ERO, D/DL 23, Thomas, Lord Dacre, An account of the Lennard family and Barony of Dacre and of the families of Belhouse and Barrett, unpublished (c.1775), 70.

12   ERO, D/DL E22, Household expenses of Francis, Lord Dacre, at Herstmonceaux, 1643-9.

13   W.G. Perrin, ed., *The Autobiography of Phineas Pett, 1630* (Naval Records Society, 1918), 21-2, 96.

14   *The Yachtsman, British Yachts and Yachtsmen*, 24.

15   W. Mathews, ed., *The Diary of Samuel Pepys* (1970), IV, 123.

16   Evelyn, *Diary*, 339.

17   Pepys, *Diary, II*, 104.

18   William Cooper, ed., *Saville Correspondence: Letters to and from Henry Saville Esq., Envoy at Paris and Vice Chamberlain to Charles II and James II*, Camden Society, 1st Series, 71 (1858), 303.

19   Pepys, *Diary*, VI, 228, III, 262.

20   Evelyn, *Diary*, 549; Greenville Collins, *Great Britain's Coasting Pilot* (1693).

21   Henry Oldenburg, ed., *Philosophical Transactions: giving some Accompt of the Present Undertakings, Studies and Labours of the Ingenious in many considerable parts of the World* (London and Oxford, 1665-77). The *Transactions* were published as private ventures by the Secretaries of the Royal Society until 1750, when they became the editorial and financial responsibility of the Society.

22   Evelyn, *Diary*, 416.

23   C.G.'t Hooft, 'The first English yachts', *Mariner's Mirror*, 5 (1919), 108-23, 116-7.

24   Clark, *History of Yachting*, 94. Presumably, in fact, second to Lord Dacre's boat.

25   Pepys, *Diary*, IX, 302, VI, 300.

26   J. Chappel, ed., *The Tangier Papers of Samuel Pepys* (Naval Records Society, 1935), 110.

27   Stephen Fisher, 'George I's progresses from Whitehall to Hanover in 1723, 1725, and 1727', *Mariner's Mirror*, 75 (1989), 371-5.

28   F.A. Dingley, 'Gwyn's Book of Ships', *Mariner's Mirror*, 7 (1921), 46-52.

29 David R. MacGregor, *Fast Sailing Ships: Their Design and Construction, 1775-1875* (1988), 16.

30 Richard Trench, *Travellers in Britain: Three Centuries of Discovery* (1990), 156.

31 Clark, *History of Yachting*, 136.

32 David Erskine, ed., *Augustus Hervey's Journal: Being the Intimate Account of the Life of a Captain in the Royal Navy Ashore and Afloat 1746-1759* (1952), 128, 67, 146, 180.

33 H.J.K. Jenkins, *Lord Orford's Voyage round the Fens in 1774* (Cambridgeshire Libraries Publications, 1987).

34 Roger North, A. Jessop, ed., *The Autobiography of the Hon. Roger North* (1887), 27-33.

35 Thomas Bowery, Richard Carnac Temple, ed., *The Papers of Thomas Bowery* (1927), 1-109.

36 John Stanley, Jane H. Adeane, ed., *The Early Married Life of Maria Josepha, Lady Stanley: with Extracts from Sir John Stanley, Praeterita* (1900), 56-60.

37 *British Yachts and Yachtsmen*, 103.

38 William Hickey, A. Spencer, ed., *Memoirs of William Hickey,1 (1749-74)* (1948), 86; *Gentleman's Magazine*, 43 (1773), 464; NLS, Ms 17624, Argyle yacht bills; Clark, *History of Yachting*, 202; *London Chronicle*, 1 Sept. 1814.

39 DRO, 1580M, Courtenay Papers, V14, Cash book 15, 1781-95; Phillips-Birt, *Cumberland Fleet*, 21.

40 Phillips-Birt, *Cumberland Fleet*, 21.

41 Royal Cornwall Gazette, 21 May, 18 June 1808.

42 C.B. Andrews, ed., *The Torrington Diaries: Containing the Tours through England and Wales of the Hon. John Byng, (Later 5th Viscount Torrington) between the years 1781 and 1794* (1934-6), 269.

43 *Hampshire Courier*, 16 Sept. 1815.

44 Clark, *History of Yachting*, 108, 202.

45 PCA. The evidence for Lord Courtenay's voyage is family tradition, based upon the simultaneous disappearance of Lord Courtenay and his yacht in 1811, coupled with his subsequent residence in New York, and the later sale of the *Dolphin's* cannon in New York.

46 DoRO, D/WLC, Letter from John Wall to E. Weld of Lulworth Castle, asking for inclusion in the crew for the voyage, 22 Feb. 1775.

47 *Morning Herald*, 3 Aug. 1809.

48 *Morning Post*, 8 Aug. 1815.

49 *Gentleman's Magazine*, 68 (1798), 717; 72 (1802), 585, 970; 76 (1807), 597; 77 (1807), 581, 684-5, 773, 781; 78 (1808), 549; 80 (1810), 175; *The Times*, 30 June 1812, 9 June 1813.

50 *Gentleman's Magazine*, 75 (1805), 585, 970.

51 Hickey, *Memoirs*, 298, 75-6, 86.

52 *Gentleman's Magazine*, 18 (1749), 377.

53 Phillips-Birt, *The Cumberland Fleet*, 17.

54 Dorothy George, *London Life in the Eighteenth Century* (1965 edn.), 267.

55 Hickey, *Memoirs*, I, 297-8.

56 *Public Advertiser*, cited by Guest and Boulton, *Memorials of the Royal Yacht Squadron*, 17-18.

57 RYS, Anon, *Rules and Orders for the Water Club of the Harbour of Cork, as established in 1720: Reprinted from an Original Copy*, undated pamphlet, origin not stated, possibly Cork Water Club. The last page contains a description of the Water Club's manoeuvres, attributed to J. Roberts, *Tour through Ireland by Two English Gentlemen* (1748), 118.

58 Clark, *History of Yachting*, 200.

59 Phillips-Birt, *The Cumberland Fleet*, 21; RTYC, Rules and Regulations of the Thames Yacht Club, 1827.

60 RTYC race sheets, 1786-1809, and notes by cups displayed at the club; *Morning Chronicle*, 19 July 1786; *The Times*, 20 July 1787, 22 June 1791, 27 June, 3 Aug. 1792, 15 July 1793, 23 July 1795, 8 May 1796, 14 July 1797, 26 July 1803, 30 June 1804, 18 July 1805, 30 July 1808; *Sporting Magazine*, July 1795, July 1796, Aug. 1796, May 1800; Clark, *History of Yachting*, 222-9.

61 *The Times*, 9 June 1788, 22 June 1791.

62 *The Times*, 4 Aug. 1795.

63 *The Times*, 18 July 1805; *Sporting Magazine*, New Series 24 (1829), 306.

64 Phillips-Birt, *The Cumberland Fleet*, 17; W. Wroth, *The London Pleasure Gardens of the Eighteenth Century* (1896), 283; *Bell's Life in London*, 29 Aug. 1824.

65 *The Times*, 3 Aug. 1792; *Bell's Life in London*, 22 Aug. 1824.

66 Clark, *History of Yachting*, 222; *Sporting Magazine*, 15 May 1800.

67 *Morning Chronicle*, 19 July 1786; *Pearce Egan's Life in London and Sporting Guide*, 28 (1824), 223.

68 Hickey, *Memoirs* 1, 298; *Gentleman's Magazine*, 19 (1749), 377; *Morning Chronicle*, 17 July 1786.

69 Drear, *Royal Yacht Squadron*, 21, 32, 35.

70 Guest and Boulton, *Memorials*, 51.

71 RYS, membership list for 1824.

72   Drear, *Royal Yacht Squadron*, 24-5, 34.
73   Drear, *Royal Yacht Squadron*, 18, 21, 32.
74   RYS, Royal Yacht Squadron Membership Lists, 1815, 1824.
75   *The Sporting Magazine*, 8 (1796), 269; *The Times*, 5 Oct. 1790, 2 Oct. 1798, 17 Sept. 1802; Drear, *Royal Yacht Squadron*, 16; Basil Greenhill, 'The schooner *Peggy*: eighteenth-century survival at the Nautical Museum, Castletown', *Journal of the Manx Museum*, 84 (1968), 68-76, 72.
76   K.V. Burns, *Plymouth Ships of War: A History of Vessels built in Plymouth, 1694-1860* (1972), 52, 72, 103-5, 117.
77   J.L. Clifford, 'Johnson's trip to Devon in 1782', in W.H. Bond, ed., *Eighteenth Century Studies: In Honor of D.F. Hyde* (New York, 1970), 3-28. This was only one of Dr Johnson's yacht expeditions. His well-known remark that 'no man will be a sailor, who has contrivance enough to get himself into jail', could not have been inspired by this excursion. It was recorded by James Boswell on 31 Aug. 1733, in his *Journal of a Tour to the Hebrides with Samuel Johnson, LL.D.* (1786): during the Hebridean tour Johnson made several sea passages, often in yachts.
78   *Exeter Flying Post*, 1 July 1767.
79   *Plymouth and Devonport Weekly Journal*, 5 Aug. 1824.
80   DRO, 1508M, V36a, loose leaves from a cash book, 1731-4, 1 Jan. 1733; V36, Sir William Courtenay's Account Book by Dormer Fynes, from 1733, 13 Jan. 1736, May 1736-Oct. 1736; PCA, Powderham Castle Estate Inventories, 1762, 1789; Tradesmen's Ledger from 1765, Worthington Brice; bill from Wells Bros. for *Dolphin 2*, June, 1787; bill from Thomas Owen for 'new yatch', 16 June 1807; account and receipt from Mr Good for sale of *Dolphin 3*, 25 April 1811; account for sale of pleasure boats, 1811; *Exeter Flying Post*, 7 Feb. 1803.
81   DRO, 1508M, V36, Sir William Courtenay's Account Book by Dormer Fynes, from 1733, 17 Jan. 1736.
82   *Exeter Flying Post*, 18 July 1763.
83   PCA, Tradesmen's Ledger from 1765, Worthington Brice account for new yacht boat built 1763; bill from Wells Bros. for *Dolphin 2*, June 1787.
84   PCA, See 45 for Lord Courtenay's voyage; Account from Mr Good for the sale of *Dolphin 3*, and recovery of his debt, 25 April 1811.
85   PCA, Powderham estate inventories, 1762 and 1789.
86   *Exeter Flying Post*, 24 Feb., 10 June 1803, 30 Aug. 1804; PCA, Tradesmen's Ledger, Worthington Brice, 6 Dec. 1768; bill from

Mr Owen, 5 March 1808; DRO, 1508M, V14, Cash Book 1768-81, 13 Nov. 1769.

87 DRO, 1508M, V36, Dormer Fynes account, 1 Jan. 1736; V36a, loose leaves from a cash book, 1731-4, 1 Jan. 1733; PCA, Powderham estate inventory, 1762; account for sale of pleasure boats, 20 July 1811.

88 DRO, 1508M, Dormer Fynes account, 14 June 1736; V36a, loose leaves from cash book, 1731-4, 9 July 1732, 11 Oct. 1733.

89 DRO, 346M, Papers of Drake of Buckland, list of debts of Sir Francis Drake at his death.

90 COR, PA/Lib/36/2, Antony House Papers, bills for Reginald Pole's pleasure boat, 1745-8.

91 WDRO, 1259/1184, Boringdon Letters, letter from Teresa Parker to Mrs Robinson, 26 July 1791.

92 *Exeter Flying Post*, 25 Sept. 1806.

93 *Exeter Flying Post*, 1 Jan., 20 May 1799.

94 *Exeter Flying Post*, 28 March 1811.

95 *Exeter Flying Post*, 23 April 1789.

96 *Exeter Flying Post*, 21 Sept. 1795.

97 *Exeter Flying Post*, 23 Sept. 1812.

98 *Hampshire Telegraph*, 30 Sept. 1811.

99 *Exeter Flying Post*, 8 April 1813.

100 *Exeter Flying Post*, 17 Feb. 1771.

101 *Exeter Flying Post*, 18 Nov. 1797.

102 *Exeter Flying Post*, 3 Aug. 1786, 20 Aug. 1779, 16 June 1791, 9 Oct. 1794, 1 May, 15 May 1800, 9 March, 25 May, 10 Aug. 1815, 26 Aug. 1819, 10 May 1820, 12 Aug. 1824, 3 Aug. 1826; *New Exeter Journal*, 25 June 1789; *Western Luminary*, 5 Oct. 1813; *Plymouth and Dock Gazette*, 9 Dec. 1814, 27 May, 2 Sept. 1815; *The Times*, 11 Aug. 1814.

103 *Exeter Flying Post*, 20 Aug. 1779.

104 *Plymouth and Dock Gazette*, 9 Dec. 1814.

105 *Exeter Flying Post*, 9 March 1815, 2 Aug. 1819.

106 *Exeter Flying Post*, 10 Aug. 1815.

107 *Exeter Flying Post*, 27 May 1815; DRO, Otterton Parish Marriage Register, 1813-37; Register of Burials, 1813-39.

108 *Exeter Flying Post*, 9 Oct. 1794, 1 May 1800, 30 Aug. 1814.

109 *Exeter Flying Post*, 18 Aug. 1775, 14 Aug. 1800, 29 July 1802, 1 Sept. 1808, 1 Sept. 1814, 7 Sept. 1815, 12 Sept. 1816, 21 Aug., 28 Aug. 1817, 12 Aug., 19 Aug., 2 Sept. 1819, 23 July, 7 Sept. 1820, 9 Sept. 1821, 25 July, 1 Aug., 15 Aug. 1822, 24 July, 31 July, 14 Aug., 28 Aug. 1823, 5 Aug., 12 Aug., 19 Aug. 1824, 21 Aug., 28 Aug. 1825, 17 Aug., 24 Aug. 1826, 26 July, 2 Aug., 9 Aug., 16

Aug. 1827; *Star*, 21 Aug. 1811; *Plymouth Weekly*, 28 July 1825; *Plymouth Herald*, 22 July 1826; *Sporting Magazine*, New Series, XXIV (1827), 298, 390.

110 *Exeter Flying Post*, 25 July 1799, 16 July 1801, 24 Sept. 1807, 1 Sept. 1808, 19 Sept. 1911, 6 Aug. 1812, July 1813; *Star*, 21 Aug. 1811; *Western Luminary*, 17 Aug. 1813, 16 Aug. 1814.

111 *Exeter Flying Post*, 9 Aug. 1821, 12 Sept. 1816.

112 Lars E. Troide, *Journals and Letters of Fanny Burney: 1768-73* (Oxford, 1988), 281-4.

113 William George Maton, *Observations Relative Chiefly to the Natural History, Picturesque Scenery and Antiquities, of the Western Counties of England, made in the years 1794 and 1796* (1797), 1, 276-7.

114 Emily J. Climenson, ed., *Passages from the Diaries of Mrs Philip Lybbe Powys* (1899), 74-5.

115 William Gilpin, *Observations on the Western Parts of England: Relative chiefly to Picturesque Beauty, to which are added a few Remarks on the Picturesque Beauties in the Isle of Wight* (1799), 230-41.

116 George Lipscomb, *A Journey into Cornwall, through the Counties of Southampton, Wilts, Dorset, Somerset and Devon: Interspersed with Remarks, Moral, Historical, Literary, Political* (1799), 200-8.

117 *Exeter Flying Post*, 20 Aug. 1789.

118 PRO, 'Records of the Registrar General of Shipping and Seamen', *Records Information*, 5 (PRO, 1991), 1.

119 Guest and Boulton, *Memorials*, 91-159.

120 *Alfred*, 25 June 1822.

121 *Exeter Flying Post*, 20 Aug. 1789.

122 PCA, Tradesmen's Ledger, Worthington Brice account, 6 Dec. 1768; account and receipt for sale of *Dolphin 3* by Mr Good, 25 April 1811.

123 DRO, 1508/M, V36, Sir William Courtenay's account book by Dormer Fynes, May-Oct. 1738.

124 PCA, Account for building *Dolphin 2*, Wells Bros., 14 June 1787.

125 DRO, 1508M, V13, Cash Book (Minority), 29 Nov. 1763.

126 DRO, 1508M, V14, Cash Book, 1768-81, 30 Nov. 1769.

127 CRO, PA/Lib/36/2, bills for Reginald Pole's pleasure boat, 1745-50.

128 PRO, C110/167, accounts of Henna and Dunn, Mevagissey; Letter from Stephen Challen to Colonel Seale, Dartmouth (dated 'Saturday'), 1823; DRO, 1292/M, contract to build a yacht, Jan. 1826, and contract for purchase of *Transit*, 1826.

129 WDRO, 1259/2/188, Borringdon Letters, letter from Anne Robinson to Mrs Robinson, 1 Sept. 1793.

130 DRO, 1508m/Devon, V15, Cash Book, 1781-95, 19 Oct., 13 Dec. 1791; 23 Oct., 25 Nov. 1790; PCA, Captain Haydon's account for *Dolphin 3*, 1811.
131 DRO, 1508M, V36, account book by Dormer Fynes, May-June 1736.
132 Burns, *Plymouth Ships of War*, 145.
133 DRO, 1508M, V36, account book by Dormer Fynes, May-June 1736; June 1737.
134 PCA, account for the sale of the *Neptune*, 23 June 1788.
135 Drear, *Royal Yacht Squadron*, 26.
136 *Exeter Flying Post*, 3 Aug. 1786; *Plymouth and Dock Gazette*, 2 Sept. 1815; *Exeter Flying Post*, 18 May 1820.
137 PCA, estate inventory, 1762; bill for *Dolphin 3* from William Manley for rope and cordage, 1809.
138 PCA, Household account book from 1795, 3 Oct. 1798.
139 CRO, PA/Lib/36.2, Bills for Reginald Pole's pleasure boat, Henry Jane for Mary Put, 27 Feb. 1746.
140 *Exeter Flying Post*, 14 July 1789.
141 *Exeter Flying Post*, 13 Oct. 1808, 5 Jan. 1809.
142 *Exeter Flying Post*, 20 June 1811.
143 *Exeter Flying Post*, 11 Sept. 1775.
144 DRO, 1508M, V15 Cash Book, 1781-95, 27 July 1786.
145 *Exeter Flying Post*, 25 July 1799, 14 Aug. 1800, 16 July 1801, 29 July 1802.
146 *Exeter Flying Post*, 11 Sept. 1775, 29 July 1802, 17 July 1800.
147 PCA, Membership List, Starcross Club.
148 Samuel Curwen, Andrew Oliver, ed., *The Journal of Samuel Curwen, Loyalist* (Harvard, 1972), 1, 543; Lady Sylvester, Edwin Welch, ed., 'Lady Sylvester's Tour', *Devon and Cornwall Notes and Queries*, XXXI (1968-70), 60-2.
149 *Exeter Flying Post*, 19 Sept. 1811.
150 *Exeter Flying Post*, 29 July 1819.
151 Drear, *Royal Yacht Squadron*, 36.
152 *Exeter Flying Post*, 9 Aug. 1821, 25 July, 1 Aug., 15 Aug. 1822, 24 July, 28 Aug. 1823, 5 Aug. 1824, 21 July, 28 July 1825, 17 Aug. 1826, 26 July, 9 Aug., 23 Aug. 1827; *Bell's Life in London*, 13 July 1823, 22 Aug. 1824; *Plymouth Herald*, 29 July 1826, 21 July 1827; *Plymouth Weekly*, 24 July 1823, 5 Aug. 1824, 24 July 1825; *Sporting Magazine*, XXIV (1827), 390.
153 *Exeter Flying Post*, 5 Aug. 1824.
154 *Plymouth Herald*, 29 July 1826.

THE EMERGENCE OF MIDDLE-CLASS YACHTING IN THE NORTH-WEST OF ENGLAND FROM THE LATER NINETEENTH CENTURY

Roger Ryan

Yachting emerged as a competitive sport in the early and mid-nineteenth century and it has ever since been burdened by images of wealth and extravagance. The massive costs of racing in large yachts have persistently acted as a barrier to entry for the vast majority of people so that the 'upper end' of the sport continues to enjoy a near unrivalled degree of exclusiveness today. For all that, participation in sailing as a recreational activity has grown very rapidly since the Second World War. The number of clubs recognised by the Royal Yachting Association – the national body for the sport – rose from 250 to 831 between 1945 and 1958, and this was followed by another surge to 1,400 by the early 1980s.[1] Moreover, before 1939 yacht racing and cruising were largely confined to coastal and river venues and were very much summer activities. The growth of clubs based on reservoirs and an increase in all-the-year-round sailing at both coastal and inland clubs have since emerged as important elements in the higher levels of participation throughout Britain. That expansion can be explained partly in terms of rising personal incomes, increased leisure time and the development of small, lightweight and relatively cheap sailing dinghies. Technological advances in protective clothing as well as a relaxation of social barriers to entry have also contributed to the greater popularity of sailing as a form of recreation since 1945.[2] It is equally important to understand how changes in the organisation and control of yachting before 1939 contributed to its post-1945 expansion. In particular, the nature of yacht racing altered significantly between the 1880s and 1914 because it changed from being a highly exclusive activity for a wealthy elite using large yachts to become a form of recreation in which middle-class influence upon the organisation of the sport was channelled through its national organising body, known as the Yacht Racing Association (YRA) until it became the Royal Yachting Association in 1952.[3]

The purpose of this paper is to show how the YRA's influence worked locally in one region, the North-West of England, by reference

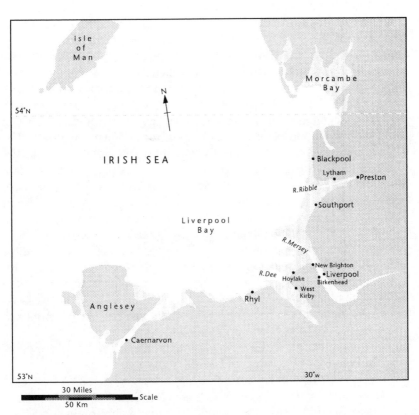

Map 1. The NORTH WEST of ENGLAND and NORTH WALES
Areas of heavy estuarine silting and sand deposits are indicated thus

to the long-established Royal Mersey Yacht Club as well as the activities of relatively new clubs within the area shown on Map 1. Quite apart from national pressures, the local history of a recreational activity such as yachting reflects the impact of specific local economic and social factors and, in this case, the nature of the various sailing waters along the main estuaries and sea-coasts of the North West. The technical and social aspects of the sport were in many respects inseparable and, while the paper inevitably has to deal with each in turn, that interdependence is a main theme of this discussion. The costs of building and maintaining a boat, for instance, had a profound influence on design decisions because they largely determined who could afford to sail. But designs also evolved in response to the conditions of local sailing waters which, as examples from the experiences of yachtsmen in the Ribble and Mersey estuaries will show, could be at least partly a product of regional economic growth and the associated political squabbles which arose from the impact of local river and port developments upon recreational amenities. The next section explains how organised yachting emerged as a middle-class activity during the late nineteenth century, with specific references to experiences in the North West. Technical changes in the sport are then discussed, again with an emphasis upon the North West because the region had a particularly strong influence on the development of small boats in what came to be known as 'one-design' classes. The final section relates these institutional and technical changes to the actual membership of local yacht and sailing clubs by considering the types of people who were able to participate and – equally significantly – those who, by virtue of their social class or because they were women, found themselves at best on the sidelines of the sport.

The Emergence of Yachting as a Middle-Class Activity

Yachting in the North West and National Trends to 1939

As late as the mid-1850s, there were still only twenty-two yacht clubs in the British Isles.[4] Those beyond southern England were confined to a handful of centres where the scale of mercantile or landed wealth could hardly be denied. In the North West, for instance, the Royal Mersey Yacht Club had stood as witness to Liverpudlian prosperity since 1844.[5] Others elsewhere included the Royal Yorkshire at Hull and Caernarvon's Royal Welsh, both dating from 1847, as well as Glasgow's prestigious Royal Northern, at Rothesay, from 1824, and the Royal Clyde at Hunter's Quay, founded in 1856. Ireland also had some eminent clubs, including the Queenstown-based Royal Cork which began in 1720. Over the next twenty years the total rose so that at least sixty-four yacht clubs had been established in the British Isles by 1874. Even this fairly modest growth was enough to prompt discussions among leading yachtsmen throughout Britain, but primarily in the South, who then formed the Yacht Racing Association (YRA) in 1875. From the start, the YRA set out to regulate British yachting. Its founding members were particularly concerned with two aspects of the sport; first, devising a system of time handicaps which would allow dissimilar yachts to compete on equal terms; secondly, establishing basic rules of sporting behaviour on the water and, where necessary, ruling on disputed member club decisions.[6] On the latter, the YRA's very clearly defined racing regulations were but part of a general framework of unwritten rules which had a strong influence upon behaviour in every 'recognised' club. Meanwhile, however, dissatisfaction with the complexity and injustices of the YRA's rating rules for yacht handicapping led to the emergence of so-called 'one-design' classes. It was in this respect, rather than at the elite end of the sport that the North West played a leading part in the development of yachting as a more affordable, and so more accessible, form of recreation for the middle-class.

The Influence of the YRA
The YRA was intent upon maintaining a high standard of 'gentlemanly' conduct upon the water and within clubhouses as participation in the sport widened. Certainly, the YRA's role extended to social background and behaviour generally. It retained control before 1914 because no new club could hope to survive for long without YRA recognition, which was only granted after a careful vetting of the new club's rule-book, membership list and racing programme. Exclusiveness and social conformity were thereby retained during the next forty years despite the fact that the number of clubs grew considerably.[7] There were already some 120 recognised British yacht clubs by the mid-1890s and this was followed by a further increase to over 200 on the eve of the First World War.[8]

The pattern of club growth in the North West reflected national trends. In 1850 there were still only three clubs in the region: the Royal Mersey, the largely defunct Royal Dee, and the Royal Welsh. As indicated earlier, all of them relied heavily upon the waters around Anglesey for their prestige events. Only two other clubs had been established even twenty years later; the Cheshire Yacht Club and the New Brighton Sailing Club. However, from 1870 to the early 1900s at least another sixteen clubs were founded in the North West.[9] The terms 'yacht' and 'sailing' club had become virtually synonymous in this context, and these new arrivals secured YRA recognition with little difficulty because they adopted the same values and rules as existing clubs and they were based firmly on the growth of middle-class recreational activity in the North West. Total membership in each club appears to have ranged between one and two hundred.[10] Allowing for multiple membership, which is known to have been extensive, that suggests a total of, at the most, some 2,000 active yachtsmen in the region during the Edwardian period.

This was certainly a notable increase in participation. It undoubtedly reflected the growing influence of rail travel in allowing those with the free time and financial means to pay the fares to reach coastal and estuary venues for summer evening or Saturday afternoon races. Southport, for instance, had an extremely strong 'Manchester' connection among the members of its two yacht clubs with the cotton textile industry being particularly well represented. Even so, a consensus clearly existed about the limits of wider involvement at this stage. In 1897, for instance, the normally enthusiastic Mersey correspondent for *Yachting World* saw little reason to welcome the arrival of a third club, the Rock Light SC, at New Brighton. With the West Cheshire and New Brighton Sailing Clubs nearby, he wrote, there was 'quite sufficient sport for that particular district, and the multiplication of clubs is not an unmixed blessing'.[11] At the same time, he and other yachting journal correspondents were equally opposed to large impersonal clubs with memberships exceeding a few hundred. In their minds, then, there were clearly limits to how far yachting could expand without threatening standards, and this continued to act as a brake on the rate of social change in the sport. At Southport, for instance, the trippers could gaze at yachtsmen from the pier with a mixture of admiration and envy. Such high visibility undoubtedly enhanced the status of yachting as a form of middle-class leisure activity, but it was also a very public demonstration of the remoteness of all forms of sailing from the day-to-day lives of even those factory workers, shopkeepers, dockers and the like who could afford a break.

None the less, the sheer pressure of demand for more and better recreation ensured that there were limits to such exclusiveness. During the 1900s, growth continued with new clubs for small centre-board craft opening at well established sailing venues in the South East, in particular, although the Rock Light example shows that the pressures were more widespread than that. Their members were initially viewed with suspicion by the YRA which feared that a sustained growth of less costly sailing would eventually open the door to artisan involvement. Even the new yachting journals seemed to hesitate in the 1890s and early 1900s because they were still prone to excessive deference towards the wealthy. For all that, their editors relied upon advertising revenue as well as sales receipts and they realised that a potential new demand existed from the 'man of moderate means' who was as likely as the wealthy elite to become a regular subscriber. At the modest rate of 3d per weekly copy, the likes of *TheYachtsman* and *Yachting World* were well within his means and he became a source of business worth attracting by offering his cause well-publicized support through their journal editorial columns. Fortunately, the YRA appreciated this and had the wisdom to make concessions to the new dinghy sailors by granting recognition to an increased number of clubs rather than risk the development of strong rival bodies. In that respect, the inter-war years witnessed a further widening of participation and less rigidity in the rules for recognising clubs.[13] For its part, the YRA succeeded in retaining firm control over both sporting and social standards as the sole national body for yachting. Compared with the frequently bitter rivalries between bodies in other sports – such as athletics, rugby and rowing[14] – this contributed towards the relatively smooth development of all aspects of British yachting after the First World War.

That much said, it is equally important to define the limits of formal participation in yachting before 1914. Diehard elements retained much influence at all levels. No club, for instance, could include 'mechanics' or 'artisans' among its members if it wanted YRA recognition.[15] Such obvious exclusiveness lost some of its edge in the inter-war years. But there is very little evidence of working class participation in the yachting activity recognised by the YRA before 1939. As in other sports like tennis and golf, this meant that the extent of democratisation was confined to those in the middle-classes who could be trusted to adopt and then support the 'Corinthian' or amateur values of the wealthy elite. As explained below, selection for club membership remained tightly controlled by committees with firm ideas about who was and who was not suitable and they were guided by the YRA's insistence that 'artisans' were not to be recruited. Indeed, similar ideas continued to influence standards of behaviour in other sectors of British sport, like tennis and golf, which recruited members from the same social background as yachting, including those with a modest income so long as they had a respectable middle-class occupation.[16] That is why the vast majority of new yacht clubs formed during the 1880s and 1890s went out of their way to emphasise their 'respectability'. All adopted hierarchies of flag officers, among whom the commodore was the most senior. Most also had a president who was chosen for his representative 'figurehead' status as a wealthy individual, preferably, but not necessarily, with an aristocratic title.

The obvious wealth and influence of the Royal Mersey's mid-nineteenth century membership will, for example, be seen later from Table 1 below, which identifies the occupations of the 101 members who were elected in 1862. Local merchants, shipowners and the professions, including marine insurance brokers, dominated what was a roll-call of Liverpool's social elite. Over the next forty to fifty years the geographical spread of the club's membership widened a little to include Manchester, as well as other parts of Lancashire and Cheshire and the coast of North Wales. However, the wealth and social standing of those elected remained beyond question. Meanwhile, a similar pattern existed in the equally prestigious but smaller Royal Welsh Yacht Club at Caernarvon, which attracted strong local gentry support as well as wealthy recruits from Liverpool and Ireland who liked to visit Anglesey.[17] And to the North from 1860, the Windermere Sailing Club – which achieved the coveted 'Royal' status in 1887 and became the Royal Windermere Yacht Club – also offered idyllic surroundings for the select few who could afford to retire to the Lakes or purchase a second home there.[18]

As indicated on Map 1, this region stretches from Caernarvon in the South to the coast by Blackpool and Fleetwood in the North. It includes the Menai Straits, the coastal resorts of North Wales and the estuaries of the Rivers Dee, Mersey and Ribble. It provides the geographical context for the following discussion; marked as it is by the limits of the influence of the Royal Windermere Yacht Club in the North and the Royal Welsh to the South. Neither of these clubs ever achieved membership totals to compare with the Royal Mersey – both remaining well below 200 before 1914 – but they did enjoy similar levels of social status. Of course, within the more rapidly expanding Royal Mersey, there were some indications of a slight widening of occupational structure, with more diversity among those in the 'professions' as well as a growing core of manufacturers. Further changes occurred during the inter-war years, with new occupations and a few members from locations beyond the North West. For all that, the high social standing of those elected remained beyond question, and the status of the Royal Mersey as by far the largest and most 'senior' local club continued to have a powerful influence upon the way in which yachting developed in the North West from the 1880s to 1939.

Clubs of such wealth and prestige as the Royal Mersey were clearly no threat to the traditions of elitism cultivated by yachtsmen in the early and mid-nineteenth century. Most of their members owned large yachts capable of lengthy voyages and they took what could at best be described as a lukewarm attitude towards smaller boats. In 1866, for instance, the Royal Mersey decided that 'yachts with moveable keels or centreboards must sail in a class by themselves'.[19] Nevertheless, the North West coastline was within easy reach of a vast and rapidly growing urban population by the late nineteenth century. There were already some two-and-a-half million people living in Lancashire and Cheshire by 1851 and this total more than doubled to nearly five-and-a-quarter million over the next fifty years. Little wonder, then, that the seaside began to figure prominently in the recreational activities of many people in the North West. On the one hand, as John Walton has explained, the Lancashire and North Wales seaside resorts were besieged by day-trippers whose sheer volume made up for their limited individual spending power as a source of profit. On the other hand, though, the same coastal towns increasingly became regular holiday venues or a home base for commuting by a middle-class which could afford the time and money for organised recreation.[20] To that extent, local yachting stood alongside golf, tennis and later motoring. Like these other activities, yachting enjoyed a reputation for exclusiveness which must in itself have attracted at least some members into local clubs.

Even so, the elite world of large yacht racing and its attendant snobbery played only an indirect part in the activities of most yachtsmen in the North West. The obvious wealth of Royal Mersey members, for instance, was never matched by the same levels of spending and commitment to yachting as existed on the Clyde or in the South. *The Yachtsman* published a massive text on the sport in 1907. Its biographical section gave profiles of some 500 of the most prominent British yachtsmen who were still active sailors. Only thirty-six of them could be said to have any real connection with the North West and they were, of course, drawn from the undeniably wealthy industrial, commercial and professional elites of Liverpool and Manchester with a few landowners and others from slightly further afield who enjoyed a similar social standing. Most, in turn, were members of the Royal Mersey which, as explained, continued to enjoy an unrivalled status as the 'senior' club in these waters.[21] For all their local wealth and influence, the absence of any really good deep coastal waters, except for those around Anglesey, greatly reduced the scope for prestige events in large yachts when compared to those in the South or on the Clyde. Silting was a widespread problem to the north of the Mersey and in the Dee, where yachtsmen at Hoylake were reporting it as a 'serious matter' for even relatively small sailing boats by 1893.[22]

That is why the Royal Mersey attracted relatively few members from beyond the North West, whereas senior clubs in other parts of Britain, particularly in the South and on the Clyde had a significant number of wealthy outport members who visited in the summer and then perhaps retired in later life to these more congenial sailing waters. By contrast, the world renowned Mersey Estuary had an extremely tricky tidal flow, with treacherous sandbanks surrounding the fairly narrow entrance channels. As the Liverpool correspondent of the *Yachting World* explained to his readers in 1894, the other large yachting centres in Britain 'are not so utterly dependent upon suitable tides'.[23] Coupled to this, as one leading Royal Mersey YC member, Dr John Hayward, commented in 1907, local yachtsmen faced the polluted 'dirty fluid' of the river and 'the smoke laden atmosphere which renders grimy our sails and gear', quite apart from the 'crowded traffic' arising from the busy port activities. Little wonder, he added, that 'if we compare our waters with the Clyde or Falmouth harbour or a few other sailing expanses, we may seem to be at a disadvantage'! Faced by such prospects, the 'big yachts won't visit us, or come to race for our pots'.[24] Dr Hayward was not one to give in. Like other Royal Mersey YC members he took considerable pride in the fact that numerous local clubs had emerged with 'brother sportsmen' who were keen to race on a regular basis even though, with the exception of the Straits Regattas held every August at Menai, the premier yachts ignored the North West.

In fact, the silting and perverse tides which were the major deterrents to visitors, proved a stimulus to local clubs and designers. The new clubs which appeared across the North West in the 1890s and 1900s were well aware of the task ahead of them. Clubs were founded, for example, along the coast from Blackpool and Lytham, through Southport and Blundellsands, and across the Mersey at Hoylake and Rhyl (see Map 1). They were beset by difficulties virtually from the day that they started. Trapped by the sand laden outflows of the Mersey, Dee and Ribble, their survival was more a tribute to persistence than logic. Sailing off these coasts was never easy. Yet these new clubs played a vital part in the success of small boat racing in the North West. Local designers produced centre-board craft – that is without a fixed keel – which were very seaworthy and particularly suited to racing or cruising along coastlines with numerous shoals. They created what can be fairly described as a thriving programme of small yacht sailing in the region from the 1890s up to 1914 which, for the most part, then survived the more trying times of the inter-war years. Above all, small yachts became very popular in the 1890s and 1900s as new clubs emerged to meet the needs of those who could not afford the cost of sailing with the likes of the Royal Mersey.

Technical Changes

One-designs

Why did one-design yachts become so popular in the later nineteenth century? The basic reason was that yachting was becoming ridiculously expensive. Prior to one-designs, racing yachts could only be compared with one another according to an estimated time handicap determined by various measurements such as waterline length, sail area, keel depth and beam. During the mid-nineteenth century, there was a high degree of conformity in designs and the relatively small number of racing yachts competed with one another on what were accepted as fair time handicaps. This cosiness was threatened in the 1860s and 1870s by American influences, as well as by advances in design theory and the growth in participation by wealthy individuals. Of course, the creation of the YRA was in itself a sign of growing concern among the yachting establishment. And there followed a near bewildering series of changes in the handicap rules from the 1880s to the 1900s. Against a background of rapid technical change and higher levels of competition, the YRA was trying to devise a formula which would achieve three, probably irreconcilable, aims; first, to include in its rating formula those yacht dimensions which could influence boat speed; secondly, to encourage seaworthy yacht designs; and, finally, to ensure that a racing yacht would retain some market value as a cruiser after its relatively short life as a top racer was over.[25]

Wealthy fanatics invariably ignored the second and third aims. They could have a new small racer, designed to exploit every possible loophole in a rule, from drawing board to water within months – eight days if it happened to be for the Duke of York! So what chance did the man of moderate means have?[26] Little wonder that many would-be competitive yachtsmen grew tired of this excessively expensive form of racing. Instead, they reasoned that if every boat was identical, costs could be controlled, newcomers would take part and the outcome of races would depend on the helmsman's skill rather than the depth of his pocket.[27] That, in sum, was – and remains – the rationale behind one-design racing. Its apparent simplicity only makes sense in a context of growth in the sport and a willingness to focus on the type of craft which are likely to be adopted in sufficient numbers to support a viable racing programme.

A Local Example: One-designs at Southport

Conditions at Southport were highly suited to the emergence of such an attitude in the late nineteenth century. The town already had a reputation as a well-to-do seaside resort, popular with the wealthy elite of Lancashire.[28] The arrival of the railway in 1855 confirmed its accessibility as the nearest point from Manchester to the sea. Furthermore, the opening of Southport Pier in 1860 and its extension to the massive length of 4,380 feet required to reach deep water, made the town increasingly attractive to yachtsmen. With the growing popularity of yachting nationally, the Southport Corinthian Yacht Club was established with a clubhouse on the Pier during the winter months of 1883-4. It was very much a 'traditional' club, with wealthy patronage and a strong interest in large yachts.[29] Among its members, though, were a number of progressive boat owners who were ready to innovate. They included Walter Scott Hayward who was already, at only thirty years of age, well-established as a wealthy Manchester merchant and an experienced yachtsman. In 1879, he had become one of the few 'amateurs' who gained a Board of Trade Certificate for yacht masters. He figured prominently in numerous yachting reports, while his membership of the Royal Mersey YC from 1883, as well as a string of other clubs in the region, leaves little doubt as to why he became one of the best-known sailors in the North West. More significantly, as *The Yachtsman* explained in 1907, he had a 'very decided genius for organisation'.[30] It was this, rather than his undoubted talents as a yachtsman, which proved particularly significant at Southport.[31]

Even more surprising is the fact that Walter Scott Hayward took the leading part in establishing the West Lancashire Yacht Club on the same Pier in 1894. Inevitably, he relied upon the practical help of key figures such as John James Bailey, formerly an Oldham engineer, who designed the West Lancashire YC's first Pierhead base and served for some eighteen months as the Club's founding honorary secretary. Scott Hayward also recruited the Southport Corinthians' flag officers into the West Lancashire YC in a well publicised demonstration of goodwill towards the new arrival. For all that, the West Lancashire YC soon outgrew its 'senior' neighbour on the Pier and survived whereas the Corinthians gave up in the 1920s. These contrasting experiences reflect the wider pattern of events in the North West as a whole. Conditions in the region were far more suited to the rapid development of one-design centre-board craft than larger keel boats. Costs apart, the former were far less likely to be deterred by the frequently shifting channels and sandbanks so typical of local waters (see Map 2). Their chief obstacle, in fact, was the prejudice of

160

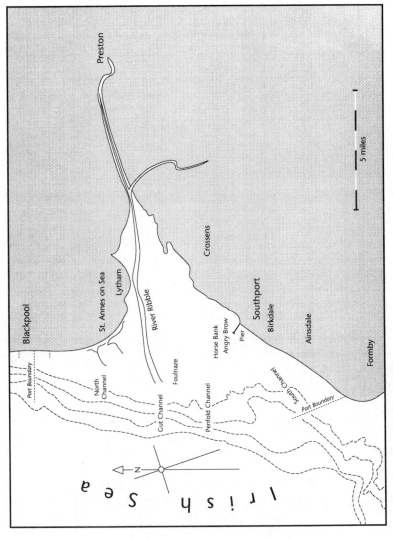

Map 2. Survey of the Ribble and Estuary, 1925.

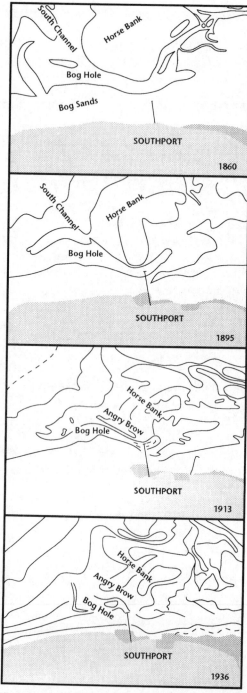

Map 3. Changes in the South Channel and 'Bog Hole' 1860 to 1936.
Source: J. Barron, 'A History of the Ribble Navigation', pp. 40-41.

traditionalists who still thought in terms of impressive deep water craft and the prestige of the grand event. Scott Hayward's contribution to yachting in the North West was marked, above all, by his successful encouragement of less costly racing, principally in one-designs but not to the exclusion of so-called 'restricted' classes of ten and twelve foot dinghies, whose owners accepted the concept of a fixed framework of basic measurement rules. On this basis, he was the central figure in the development of small boat racing not only at Southport but also in new clubs such as those at Rhyl and Hoylake as well as across the Ribble at Lytham.[32]

Quite apart from the undeniable influence of their low cost, there was a specifically local reason why the new emphasis on one-designs proved particularly successful at Southport before 1914. The point is that Southport became an increasingly difficult location for fixed-keel yachts in the late nineteenth century. Admittedly, the Pier reached out into a stretch of deep water known, with a mixture of affection and despair, as the 'Bog Hole'. A reliable survey in 1882 found that at low tide its deepest point was still an impressive 52 feet, while a stretch of water deeper than 30 feet extended 1,000 yards on either side of the Pierhead, with a width of up to 400 yards. At this stage, then, the Bog Hole could take vessels of any size, offering deep water safety to boats at anchor even in a heavy storm. Map 3, however, indicates in diagramatic form how the Bog Hole was already past its heyday when the Southport Corinthians began their sailing. This area of the Ribble Estuary was notorious for its shifting channels and sandbanks. Furthermore, the prevailing south-westerly wind frequently brought damaging storms, particularly from October to May, and left the Pier highly vulnerable as a base for any yacht club. Add to that the persistent notoriety of piers as fire risks, and one is left wondering why anyone bothered to found a yacht club on Southport Pier despite the town's many attractions as an up-market seaside resort! Even by 1894, the Bog Hole was silting up rapidly. Most impartial observers attributed this largely, if not entirely, to the development of the Port of Preston. From 1890, Preston Corporation had been developing training walls in the Ribble Channel to enable ocean-going vessels to reach its new dock. As Map 2 indicates, this work continued over the next thirty years, often with considerable delays when funds ran out. By the late 1890s the walls had reached the point where they were directing virtually all of the Ribble outflow away from the South Channel. The loss of scouring had a drastic effect upon the Bog Hole which gradually began to fill in (Map 3). By the first decade of the century the steamers which brought the bulk of the Southport Pier Company's revenue had difficulty reaching its landing stages and

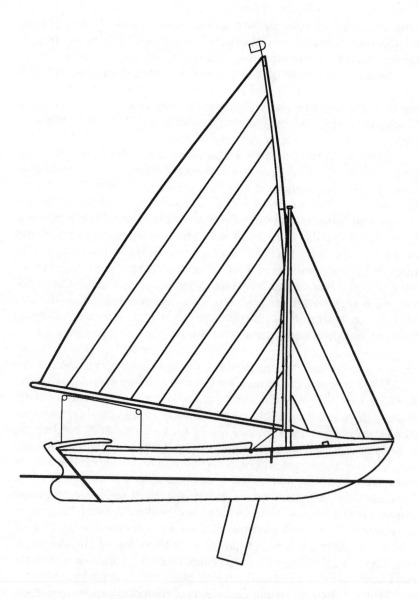

Fig. 1. Profile of the Seabird class one-design.

their services were eventually discontinued in the 1920s. Meanwhile, large yachts found the Bog Hole increasingly unsuitable as a mooring. Only the small one-design craft could continue with relatively few difficulties before 1914, and they alone provided the West Lancashire YC with a racing fleet in the inter-war years.[33]

Much was made of the political efforts to oppose Preston Corporation's plans in the 1890s and 1900s. Southport could certainly muster an impressive array of local political leaders, as well as the fishing fleet and business interests, including the Pier Company directors and the owners of the various pleasure steamers. Having no real political influence, both yacht clubs tied themselves to this alliance of local interests. But it was completely outmanouevred by Preston Corporation, which could count on the influence of Lancashire's cotton and coal wealth to back it up. One irony of the situation was that many of the leading yachting families at Southport derived their own wealth from these same sources in the heart of industrial Lancashire. Probably, their protests on behalf of Southport's commercial and recreational interests were sincere. Even so, they had little to lose. Their cotton mills continued to do well until 1914, and they were often members of the Royal Mersey YC as well. On balance, then, it is fair to say that the prospects for local political influence upon this issue were very poor from the start.[34]

Meanwhile, though, Scott Hayward deserves particular credit for the introduction of one-design sailing at Southport and in the North West generally. Indeed between the 1880s and early 1900s, when he switched his interest to racing motor boats, he was widely recognised in the yachting press as one of the most prominent yachtsmen in the region. One of his designs, the Seabird class, which he jointly produced with an electrical engineer named Herbert Baggs in 1898, still thrives in the North West today. Its importance as a relatively cheap route into yachting was recognised from the start. An earlier one-design by Scott Hayward, in 1894, had an overall length of 23 feet 5 inches. It had a centreboard and was an excellent sea boat, highly suited to the difficult sandbanks and channels around Southport. However, the boat cost £60 and its design began to be modified within a year of its first appearance so that it soon became more expensive to build and sail. In fact, only about a dozen were ever built and the escalating costs of various modifications to ballast and sail plan defeated the object of having a one-design. By contrast, the Hayward and Baggs 1898 Seabird design had clearly benefitted from this object lesson.

At 20 feet overall, the Seabird shared the same yacht-like profile of the earlier design (see Figure 1). But costs were strictly limited to

£35. Moreover, the boats were built in pairs by an approved builder and each new owner was allocated his Seabird by lots. The strict rules for the Seabird class have barely changed since then. Even in 1939, costs were limited to £100 and every part of the unchanged design continued to be rigidly specified. The outcome is that the class still has sixty-six boats in it today and racing continues on the original one-design principles. Furthermore, George Cockshott, a Southport solicitor and yachtsman, designed the even cheaper Star class, 16 feet 9 inches, dinghy in 1906. Costs were restricted to £32 and the same kind of strict rules have been retained, with the class having moved to the West Kirby SC where a fleet of twelve Stars continues to race and cruise today. The complex modern commercial environment which has evolved in British yachting relies heavily upon thriving one-design classes which continue to be based upon the principles established by innovators like Scott Hayward a century ago.[35]

At first, older clubs in the North West were reluctant to accept these new ideas. The West Lancashire YC met with some resistance in 1896 when it called a joint meeting of local clubs sailing one-designs in an attempt to coordinate their racing and so encourage more competition between clubs. In a fit of pique, the Southport Corinthians declined to send anyone despite the fact that their clubrooms were in the same building! But the Corinthians suffered for their tardiness because other representatives from the clubs at Hoylake, Rhyl, Lytham and Fleetwood all attended this, the first joint meeting in the North West, and agreed 'as to dates for matches for the coming season'.[36] The outcome was a coordinated programme of eighteen inter-club races for one-design classes to be held at four different venues in the North West. It is not hard to imagine the irritation felt by the Southport Corinthians when their members read about the agreement in the *Yachting World*, in a report which concluded that 'as no representative attended from the Corinthian Club, nothing could be done with regard to their fixtures for this class',[37] that is their one-designs.

To their credit, the Southport Corinthians had the sense to realise that change was inevitable. Rather than face isolation, they sent someone to the next meeting and then took part in a few of these inter-club events throughout the years before the First World War. However, a far more significant change in this respect came in 1911. After years of delay, the Royal Mersey YC decided that 'it was advisable to get a small class started next season'.[38] The influence of newer clubs in the North West had clearly reached the Royal Mersey. A good many of its more active members also belonged, like Scott Hayward a decade earlier, to clubs such as the New Brighton SC and the West Lancashire YC, where they could not have failed to recognise how one-design sailing was stimulating new interest in yachting without the lowering of social standards which many diehards had still regarded as the main drawback of widening access to the sport in the 1880s and 1890s.

Costs certainly figured prominently in the Royal Mersey's decision to go for a 23-feet one-design which became known as the Rivers class. A Royal Mersey committee reported: 'that such boats are good value at the price of £50'. And though opposed in principle to one design, 'having regard to ... the desirability of having an inexpensive boat', they gave the plans their full support. Once committed, they followed the same rigorous rules as other Merseyside one-designs 'in order to obtain complete uniformity'. Furthermore, each yacht was kept to a maximum of three crew when racing and they all had to be amateurs.[39] Together with the overlap in local club membership, especially at flag officer level so far as the newer clubs were concerned, such decisions helped to create a sense of a 'region' in yachting terms in a way which had not existed even twenty years earlier.

More specifically, the Southport example shows how the emphasis upon relatively cheap one-designs enabled the West Lancashire YC to fully participate in the growing number of class races in the North West. Within two years of its foundation, for instance, the West Lancashire YC had secured YRA recognition and this had given its committee the authority required to initiate the regular pre-season meetings of those clubs in the North West with an interest in one-designs; an idea which marked a further step towards wider participation and higher standards of competition. The one-design fleets of smaller yachts were absolutely essential to this development. They strengthened the links between clubs in the region and these were further enhanced by the growing practice of multiple club membership adopted by the region's leading yachtsmen. And as the new clubs found their feet they were readily accepted into this local 'fraternity' – a term frequently used within yachting at the time – of yachtsmen. Apart from shared racing programmes, local yachtsmen met at a growing number of social events ranging from their formal annual dinners to more frequent 'hot-pot' suppers and 'smoking concerts'. To this extent the growth of middle-class participation in the male-dominated circle of yacht cruising, racing and socialising in the North West – as elsewhere in Britain – was marked by a considerable uniformity under the guidance of 'senior' clubs locally and the YRA from London. It also led to more explicit rules for behaviour on the water, above all when racing, which were coupled with tacit assumptions about what type of person should be allowed to join a yacht club and how they should conduct themselves after they had become members.

The Social Aspects of Yacht Club Membership

The Ban on Artisans
For a start, the ban on working men – as 'artisans' – reflected a widespread fear in middle-class sporting circles of their physical strength and skills which might prove an advantage when competing against true 'Corinthians' who were amateurs in every sense, with no financial interest in the outcome of their sporting activity. Rugby, athletics, rowing, cricket and golf were among other sports faced by this dilemma.[40] Fears that corruption would arise as a result of organised gambling upon individual performances might have partially justified this attitude, especially in the environment of mutual suspicion between 'artisan' and middle-class sportsmen. Even so, the overriding influence was simply a form of snobbery which sought to project the social barriers of Victorian society into the growing world of sport. Of course, the influence of public schools and the universities at Oxford and Cambridge gave such 'athleticism' a moral approval which served to enhance the image of these activities in the minds of those middle-class merchants, stockbrokers and various professionals who formed the core membership in those clubs recognised by the YRA before 1914.[41]

Amateur yachtsmen certainly had every reason to fear the expertise of the men who sailed in the numerous fishing fleets which could still be found scattered around the British coastline in the late nineteenth century. In the North West, as elsewhere, trawler skippers and lifeboatmen took to the sea throughout the year. They understood the vagaries of local channels, tides and currents particularly well and would have been formidable competitors in any yacht race. Of course, many were hired as paid hands in larger yachts during the summer and played a key part in this form of racing even though the YRA rules prevented them from taking the helm. That never presented any difficulty because such yachts were also well beyond the means of most middle-class members, and there was little chance of even the most prosperous 'artisan' ever being able to afford one.[42]

The problems came when clubs began to race the smaller one-designs because they cost far less to build and maintain, while they could be sailed either single-handed or with one amateur crew. Cost barriers to entry therefore fell to bring yachting within the means of a few artisans, particularly boatbuilders and sailmakers or fishing vessel owners, raising the possibility – albeit remote – that they would compete on their own account rather than as paid hands. In 1907, for example, the newly formed Blackpool & Fleetwood Sailing Club elected David Leadbetter, the Fleetwood Lifeboat coxswain, to the membership. However, an influential member who was also in the Royal Mersey Yacht Club advised the Blackpool & Fleetwood SC committee not to allow artisans to join. As the senior club in the North West, the RMYC was virtually duty-bound to follow the YRA's guidelines, and it was through the local link of multiple club membership that this social influence filtered to all other recognised clubs in the region. The Blackpool & Fleetwood Committee obediently resolved 'that as an amateur Club it was not advisable to admit as members men who were engaged in the occupation of boatmen'.[43] David Leadbetter, in turn, accepted the decision without protest: 'when the situation was fully explained to him' a week later, he obligingly 'agreed to withdraw his application for membership' and the club refunded his subscription.[44] An occasional reminder such as this proved adequate in a society where the boundaries between social classes were still firmly defined in terms of occupation and income.

Women and Yachting

Social class apart, late Victorian and Edwardian yachting was, like many other sports, dominated by men. A few very good women helms managed to succeed on the water, but they still found the shore institutions of clubhouse, annual general meeting and annual dinner generally closed to them. The scope for female involvement was therefore well controlled by the institutional arrangements which underpinned the organisation of yachting in Britain. Some clubs still refused to have women members. But these were in the minority and it was the norm – certainly by the turn of the century in the North West – to accept 'Lady Members', while confining their formal influence to a subordinate role on a so-called 'Ladies Committee'. Clubs in the North West were no better or worse than others throughout Britain in this respect. Only eleven women were named among the 1907 review of 500 prominent 'yachtsmen' in Britain referred to earlier, and of these only Gladys Scott Hayward, daughter of Walter Scott Hayward, had links with Merseyside.[45]

Perhaps this hardened minority gained the respect which they deserved, but male attitudes towards yachtswomen in general before 1914 appear to the modern observer as extremely patronising. For all that, women beyond the wealthy few listed among the top 500 yachtsmen sometimes got the chance to demonstrate such a high level of skill that their talents could not be ignored. In one sense, the customary end-of-season 'ladies' race, which persists in many clubs today, proved a mixed blessing in this respect. Men watched women handling yachts very competently, while through the pages of the yachting press they could not avoid the obvious point that there was, to quote a 1905 *Yachting World* report from Southport, no shortage of 'fair skippers' well able to compete effectively with male helms.[46] On a growing number of occasions in the North West, as elsewhere in Britain, some common sense prevailed, not least because women were a necessary part of the smooth functioning of any amateur club, especially in clubs such as those formed in the late Victorian and Edwardian periods which were so firmly rooted in the ranks of the middle-class from a wide range of professional and business occupations. For such true 'Corinthians', the gradual rise in wages for people who worked in service or as paid hands on boats tended to rule out their employment on a regular basis. The further costs of employers' liability insurance and, then, national insurance for sickness benefits added to potential labour costs in the decade before the First World War. Add to that, the post-war surge in wage rates lasting until the early 1920s, and it is hardly surprising that club membership for the wives, daughters and girlfriends of yachtsmen gradually came to be viewed in more favourable terms during this period.[47]

The potential of lady members for a worthy role as jib trimmers and sandwich cutters is evidenced in the 'hearty vote of thanks' which these efforts frequently gained in club minutes. Women could make some gains on the water through this means because they began to take a greater part in events such as the so-called 'crews' race, an annual event common to most clubs in which less experienced sailors were given an opportunity to compete with one another. Even then, reports tended to emphasise that a win with a woman at the helm owed much to the guiding presence of the male crew, rather than to the potential ability of a female who had probably turned out in all weathers to handle the jib and spinnaker of the same boat with little recognition.

Given an equal chance, in fact, the prospects for yachtswomen were better than for their counterparts in other middle-class sports like tennis, golf and the 'man's world of rowing'.[48] In these and similar activities, physical strength ensures that the male-female divide remains at most competitive levels even today. That does not need to be the case in yachting where skill can be the determining factor if an appropriate design of boat is used in races. In practice, though, yachting at all levels continues to be dominated by men and the reasons for this lie as much in the development of the social side of the sport as in the handling of boats. Of course, the most blatant forms of discrimination have now all but disappeared in Britain. However, this has largely been due to pressures for change which have led to a greater democratization of middle-class sport generally since the Second World War. Some twenty years earlier, it is true that the First World War did much to throw the position of all women in British society open to far more debate. Many middle-class women in particular, and they were the norm for yacht club membership, had gained new confidence and a sense of status from the war which had shown that they could secure economic independence in a way which had been denied them in Edwardian society.

However, even these substantial changes did little more than briefly shake the foundations of the accepted principle that yacht clubs were a male preserve into which women were sometimes 'allowed' on sufferance and in no sense as equals. Within the North West, for instance, both the West Kirby SC and the West Lancashire YC were adopting what seems to have been normal practice when they continued to exclude female members from their main clubhouse and denied them a formal say in running the club until after the Second World War.[49] Meanwhile, the ailing Lytham YC stuck to its original principles and remained without women members, despite being well aware by 1937 that the newly founded Lytham St Annes Motor Boat Club 'was more attractive with mixed membership and much activity ashore and afloat compared with the staid Victorian atmosphere of the Yacht Club'.[50] There seems to have been remarkably little resentment, at least publicly, from women within yacht clubs or on the fringes of the sport. Most male members had other 'club' interests, including golf, tennis, motoring, the Conservative party and strong masonic links. Such a range of activities figured in the lives of middle-class men in the North West as elsewhere in British society during the inter-war years and yachting fitted easily into this complex web of local friendships, business and leisure activities.

Yacht Club Membership in the North West

Entry to this exclusive world was guarded by the various yacht and sailing club committees with as much care as their counterparts, sometimes the same group of people, at the golf or tennis club. As examples, the analyses of occupational structure among yacht club members in Tables 1 and 2 confirm the extent to which clubs in the North West retained very tight membership controls throughout the period to 1939, even at times when this meant that recruitment fell off.

Of course, the Royal Mersey YC continued to attract many of the wealthiest and most influential individuals from the professions, industry and commerce throughout the region. Taking the period 1899 to 1939, during which the Royal Mersey maintained a continuous register of candidates for election to the club, Table 1 indicates the predominance of certain groups of occupations throughout the period. There had been some notable changes since the mid-nineteenth century, when the huge influence of local mercantile wealth is obvious from the 1862 review. Most of these early members simply called themselves 'merchants', while many of those in group 3 were marine underwriters. At this stage, also, the Royal Mersey was principally a Liverpool yacht club. By the late-Victorian and Edwardian period, however, its role as the senior club in the North West is clearly evident from the presence of manufacturers, some landowners, and of merchants and professionals from throughout the region. There are many examples, as mentioned earlier, to show that multiple club membership was very common. Those who could afford it, valued the right to call themselves a member of the 'Royal' Mersey YC, which entitled them to fly the prestigious blue ensign, even when sailing with their local clubs at Southport, on the Dee or, say, off New Brighton.

Table 1
Royal Mersey Yacht Club: Occupations of Members Elected
1862, 1899-1914 and 1915-1939

Occupation Group	Numbers of Members Elected		
	1862	1899-1914	1915-1939
1	2	31	22
2	2	12	16
3	13	115	154
4	2	48	40
5	69	108	92
6	0	37	35
7	0	1	0
8	11	46	124
9	2	34	8

Occupation Group	Percentages in Each Occupational Group		
	1862	1899-1914	1915-1939
1	2.0	7.2	4.5
2	2.0	2.8	3.3
3	12.9	26.6	31.4
4	2.0	11.1	8.2
5	68.3	25.0	18.7
6	-	8.6	7.1
7	-	0.2	-
8	10.9	10.7	25.3
9	2.0	7.9	1.6

Group 1 Legal; 2 Medicine, including dental surgeon; 3 Other professional including military officer, surveyor, banker, accountant, professor, 'clerk'; 4 Manufacturers, including brewer, shipbuilder; 5 Merchants, including newspaper proprietor, shipping agent, shipowner, cotton broker, timber broker, wood broker, yarn salesman; 6 Engineers; 7 Retail owners; 8 Others, including student, apprentice, 'gentleman', automobile agent, 'spinster', 'married woman'; 9 Not known.

Sources: 1862, RMYC, 'Minute Book of the Secretary'; 1899-1939, RMYC, 'Candidates for Election'.

Table 2
West Lancashire Yacht Club:
Known Occupations of Members, 1894-1939

Occupational Group	Numbers in Each Group for Periods Shown		
	1894-1919	1920-1939	1894-1939
1	3	2	5
2	7	3	10
3	15	14	29
4	7	4	11
5	10	18	28
6	4	0	4
7	1	3	4
8	11	2	13

Occupational   Percentages in Each Group for Periods Shown
Group

Occupational Group	1894-1919	1920-1939	1894-1939
1	5.2	4.4	4.8
2	12.1	6.5	9.6
3	25.9	30.4	27.9
4	12.1	8.7	10.9
5	17.2	39.1	26.9
6	6.9	-	3.9
7	1.7	6.5	3.9
8	19.0	4.4	12.5

For occupations in each group, see Table 1.

Sources: WLYC, Members' Yearbooks, 1914, 1915, 1919, 1922-4, 1928, 1933; Southport Reference Library, various Southport and Lancashire Local Directories 1880-1937, as listed in R.J. Ryan, *WLYC*, pp.148-9.

As might be expected, there were some notable changes within each group during the inter-war years. These owed far more to the wider structural development of the local economy than to any lowering of the social barriers to entry. Whereas, for instance, merchants and manufacturers from the cotton and shipping sectors still predominated in groups 4 and 5 for the Royal Mersey YC up to 1914, along with a core of medical and legal men in groups 1 and 2, the new faces after the First World War included those in occupations, such as brewer and manufacturing chemist, who were much less in evidence within group 4 before 1918. Within the professions, largely covered by groups 1 to 3, and the 'engineers' in group 6, there were also some notable changes in the importance of certain occupations. Of course, the Royal Mersey, like other yacht clubs, continued to attract a steady stream of doctors, surgeons and dentists throughout the period. Solicitors and barristers, were of similar importance, and it is clear that many individuals from these occupations regarded yachting and the associated social life as a very attractive option. Meanwhile, the diversification of the professions generally in Britain is reflected in the growth of membership among those in group 3 for the Royal Mersey YC.

During the 1920s and 1930s, apart from some retired military officers, who probably reflect the abnormal conditions created by the Great War, the most prominent new faces included a variety of

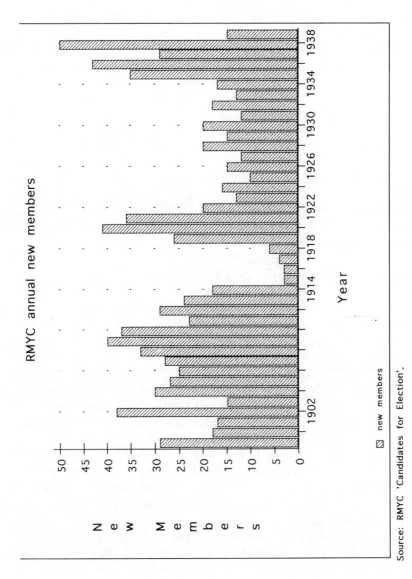

Figure 2. RMYC Annual New Members.

'managers' and 'directors' who might well have identified themselves by a specific trade, particularly cotton, before 1914. Others now include 'inspectors' and people who were civil servants. Yet another variable was the term 'salesman' which appears to have been used with far less hesitancy during the inter-war years than previously, and has been included in group 5 as if it was clearly being used by someone who would have worked in the same circles as merchants on equal terms. John Heyes is a good example. As a wealthy Manchester yarn salesman he belonged to the West Lancashire YC before 1914, and during the war he also joined the newly formed Manchester Cruising Association which aimed to encourage yachting 'and promote social intercourse between amateur sailing men in the Manchester district'.[51] Meanwhile, he was elected to the Royal Mersey YC in 1917. As the owner of the 37-ton yawl, *Lesbia*, and 10-ton auxiliary cutter, *Victoria*, he became Commodore of the West Lancashire YC from 1923 to 1931,[52] a position of influence within the North West which was typical of the route by which Royal Mersey standards reached less 'senior' clubs and maintained a common level of values within the sport.

Meanwhile, for all the changes just described, cotton and shipping wealth also proved remarkably resilient, despite the impact of the inter-war depression years upon Britain's export sectors. Every candidate for election had to undergo an interview by the Royal Mersey committee after the club secretary had secured detailed confidential references from at least two existing Royal Mersey members. Probing questions about evidence of financial circumstances and standards of social behaviour had to be addressed in these references and it is clear that initial screening procedures were rigorous and effective. Very few candidates failed to get in after their names had gone through this process to reach the Committee's list which was put before the members at large.[53]

All those joining the Royal Mersey YC therefore came from the same well-to-do social backgrounds as the existing membership. Consistency was retained despite the fluctuations in annual recruitment during the Edwardian period identified in Figure 2. Then, the wartime slump in new members and subsequent recovery was entirely consistent with national trends, not least because all racing to speak of had been suspended during the hostilities. The intakes during the 1920s and early 1930s were a reflection of a generally tight period for British yachting. The decision to introduce a one-design class from 1911, probably brought some benefits in the inter-war years because the significant growth in group 8 recruitment included 'schoolboys', undergraduates and apprentices in well-to-do occupations, all indicative of wider family involvement within the same social class. Furthermore, a very notable point about the Royal Mersey and other yacht clubs in the North West continued to be their highly localised membership. Only a tiny proportion of the Royal Mersey's membership, for example, came from outside the North West. That, in turn, is probably why there were relatively few newcomers at a time when the region's key sectors, cotton, shipping and related activities like coal mining, were facing a severe depression.

Records for the other local yacht clubs cannot compare with the detail which has survived at the Royal Mersey YC. However, an analysis of various yearbooks for the West Lancashire YC as shown in Table 2, shows a similar pattern of middle-class involvement. The earlier books, together with supporting evidence, show the importance of Southport as either a residence or visiting place for Lancastrian industrialists and merchants. Meanwhile, its 'up-market' tone is reflected in the substantial core of professional men, with lawyers, medical men, surveyors and accountants figuring prominently from the start and continuing to do so during the inter-war years. As might be expected, local businessmen of more modest means who would not have been regarded as suitable – on financial and social grounds – for membership of the Royal Mersey were accepted by the West Lancashire YC, as at most other local clubs, and by this means they were able to sail in the one-designs which continued to dominate the racing calendars at places like Southport and West Kirby.

Conclusion

This pattern of social uniformity, with a modest but notable degree of relaxation of the barriers to entry, could also be found elsewhere in Britain. John Lowerson refers to the Humber Yawl Club with a membership of about 120 in 1913. These local solicitors, merchants and other commercial men thoroughly enjoyed their 'annual round of smoking concerts, dinners and festivities to foster out of season spirits'. Their social life was, he writes, 'almost as far from that of the Royal Yacht Squadron as it is possible to imagine'.[54] His point emphasises the changes which had occurred since the 1880s even though the lavish elitism of the Royal Yacht Squadron and its kind persisted. It must also be remembered that the members of new yacht clubs, like those at Hull and in the North West, knew little or nothing of the poverty which dominated the lives of the vast majority of people in Edwardian and inter-war Britain whose occupations and low incomes placed them at best in the 'artisan' class so feared by yacht club membership election committees. In the North West, as elsewhere, it was the increasingly confident and prosperous members of the middle-class who provided the new element in British yachting. By adopting the codes of conduct of the established elite clubs, these newcomers ensured that any scope for change remained firmly controlled in terms of social class and gender. Even so, their arrival on the scene opened the way for future growth in yachting during the inter-war years and, above all, after 1945 because they were the driving force behind the introduction and widespread adoption of one-design classes. It was also a growth which incorporated rather than superseded the established clubs such as the Royal Mersey which continued to exercise a strong influence upon the conduct of yachting, including competitive racing, throughout the North West. Indeed, the Royal Mersey's cautious but positive responses to innovations by other local clubs helps to explain why the sport has thrived in a region where geography and climate combine to create conditions which are far from favourable for yachting.

ACKNOWLEDGEMENTS

I would like to thank the Commodores of the West Lancashire Yacht Club and the Royal Mersey Yacht Club for giving me access to their records. My thanks also to Gavin Allan Wood, a Lecturer in Computing at Southport College, who produced the maps and the drawing of a Seabird one-design used in this article.

NOTES

1   G. Fairley, *Minute by Minute. The Story of the Royal Yachting Association, 1875-1982* (RYA, 1983), 137-8.
2   J. Fisher, *Sailing Dinghies* (Southampton, 1961, 4th edn.), 4-19; R.J. Ryan, *The West Lancashire Yacht Club, 1894-1994* (Preston, Carnegie, 1993) (hereafter *WLYC*), 71, 114-6.
3   Fairley, *Minute by Minute*, 1-52, 115; Ryan, *WLYC*, 2-6, 11-14; J. Lowerson, *Sport and the English Middle Classes* (Manchester, 1993), 50-3.
4   *The Yachtsman* (hereafter *YM*), 23 May 1891, 92; *Yachting World* (hereafter *YW*), 10 Oct. 1907, 269, give estimates of early growth in club numbers.

5   J.D. Hayward, *A Short History of the Royal Mersey Yacht Club, 1844-1907* (Liverpool, 1907) (hereafter *RMYC*), 19-29.

6   Fairley, *Minute by Minute*, 1-3.

7   Fairley, *Minute by Minute*, 44-5; J. Lowerson, *Sport*, 50-3; Ryan, *WLYC*, 2-6.

8   Annual lists of clubs were given in Lloyds Register of Yachts, which began in 1878. Summaries of growth in the period appeared in *YM*, 23 May 1891, 92; *YW*, 10 Oct. 1907, 269.

9   *Ibid*; J.Millar, *Anything But Sailing. A History of the West Kirby Yacht Club* (Hoylake, 1985), xv, 36-7.

10   Ryan, *WLYC*, 4-5.

11   *YW*, 19 March 1897, 323.

12   See example in *YW*, 4 March 1909, 106, on large club membership.

13   Fairley, *Minute by Minute*, 61-9.

14   J. Crump, 'Athletics', 49; C. Dodd, 'Rowing', 286-7; G. Williams, 'Rugby', 313, all in T. Mason, ed., *Sport in Britain. A Social History* (Cambridge, 1989).

15   B. Heckstall-Smith, ed., *Dixon Kemp's Manual of Yacht and Boat Sailing* (10th edition, London, 1904), 598.

16   J. Lowerson, 'Golf', 200-1, 204-5; H. Walker, 'Tennis', 251, both in T. Mason, ed., *Sport in Britain*.

17   Anon, *British Yachts and Yachtsmen* (London, 1907), 516-7.

18   O.M. Westall, 'The retreat to Arcadia: Windermere as a select residential resort in the late nineteenth century', in O.M. Westall, ed., *Windermere in the Late Nineteenth Century* (University of Lancaster, 1991), 38,42.

19   J.D. Hayward, *RMYC*, 30.

20   J.K. Walton, *The English Seaside Resort. A Social History, 1750-1914* (Leicester, 1983),1-73.

21   Anon, *British Yachts and Yachtsmen*, 363-490.

22   *YM*, 7 Dec. 1893, 95.

23   *YW*, 14 Dec. 1894, 628.

24   J.D. Hayward, *RMYC*, 11-12.

25   H.C.Folkard, *The Sailing Boat. A Treatise on Sailing Boats and Small Yachts* (6th edition, London, 1906), 233-326; J. Irving, *The King's 'Britannia'. The Story of a Great Ship* (London, ?1936), 21-35; A. Viner, *A History of Rating Rules for Yachts, 1854-1931*. Maritime Monographs and Reports, No. 41 (National Maritime Museum, 1979), 2-15.

26   Viner, *Rating Rules*, 12.

27   H.C. Folkard, *Sailing Boat*, 233-7; Linton Hope, 'The evolution of the small rater', *YW*, Aug. 1898, Cowes Week Supplement.

28   Walton, *English Seaside Resort*, 160-4, 170-1.
29   Ryan, *WLYC*, 1-2, 6-10, 20-1.
30   Anon, *British Yachts and Yachtsmen*, 402.
31   Ryan, *WLYC*, 64-7.
32   Ryan, *WLYC*, 30-9.
33   J. Barron, *A History of the Ribble Navigation. From Preston to the Sea* (Preston, 1938), 40-4, 100-7, 121-2, 170-1, 450-2; J. Dakres, *The Last Tide. A History of the Port of Preston, 1835-1981* (Preston, 1986), 101-6, 115, 149-66, 190-3, 202-5; Ryan, *WLYC*, 15, 19-20, 24-7.
34   Ryan, WLYC, 24-7, 59-63, 67-70.
35   *Ibid.*, 45-9, 80-5.
36   *YW*, 24 Jan. 1896, 236.
37   *Ibid.*, 31 Jan. 1896, 247.
38   *RMYC*, 'Minute Book of the Secretary of the Royal Mersey Yacht Club, 1862 to 1913', 14 Nov. 1911.
39   *Ibid.*
40   J. Crump, 'Athletics', 49-51; J. Williams, 'Cricket', 119-20; J. Lowerson, 'Golf', 188-9, 195-6; C. Dodd, 'Rowing', 276-85; G. Williams, 'Rugby', 313; all in T. Mason, ed., *Sport in Britain*.
41   P. Bailey, *Leisure and Class in Victorian England* (London, 1987), 72-3, 83-5, 136, 139-40.
42   R. Simper, *Victorian and Edwardian Yachting from Old Photographs* (London, 1978), 1-3; *YW*, 18 May 1911, 349-50.
43   Lancashire Record Office, Blackpool & Fleetwood Sailing Club, Minutes, DDX 734 1/1, 7 April 1908; 22 April 1908.
44   *Ibid.*, 4 May 1908.
45   Anon, *British Yachts and Yachtsmen*, 363-490.
46   *YW*, 13 July 1905, 41.
47   See, for example, *YM*, 27 April 1899, 233; *YW*, 13 Jan. 1910, 10; *YW*, 14 Dec. 1911, 466. Employers' liability and then National Insurance costs appear to have been of widespread concern among yacht owners in the Edwardian period.
48   Lowerson, 'Golf', 204-8; H. Walker, 'Tennis', 260-3, 271-2; Dodd, 'Rowing', 298; all in T. Mason, ed., *Sport in Britain*.
49   Millar, *West Kirby YC*, 475-7.
50   J. Kennedy, *Lytham Yacht Club. Centenary, 1889-1989* (Lytham Yacht Club, 1989), 18.
51   Anon, *Manchester Cruising Association Season, 1918* (MCA, 1918), 5.
52   Anon, *Manchester Cruising Association Season, 1918* 'List of Members'; RMYC, 'Candidates for Election'; WLYC, Yearbooks, 'Seasons' 1914-28.
53   Various letters filed with RMYC, 'Candidates for Election'.

54   Lowerson, *Sport and the English Middle Classes*, 53.

Notes on Contributors

John Travis is an Occasional Lecturer in Social History in the Department of Economic and Social History, University of Exeter.

John K. Walton is Professor of Modern Social History at the University of Lancaster.

Paul Thornton is Deputy Director of the Institute of Cornish Studies, University of Exeter.

Nigel Morgan is Senior Lecturer in Leisure and Tourism, University of Wales Institute, Cardiff.

Janet Cusack is a member of the Centre for Maritime Historical Studies, University of Exeter.

Roger Ryan is Head of the Faculty of General Education at Southport College, Lancashire.

Stephen Fisher is a former Co-Director of the Centre for Maritime Historical Studies at the University of Exeter, and is now an Honorary Research Fellow in the Centre.